1972 Farm Journal
A Back-to-the-Land Movement Story

OAKES PLIMPTON

iUniverse, Inc.
Bloomington

1972 Farm Journal
A Back-to-the-Land Movement Story

iUniverse books may be ordered through booksellers or by contacting:

iUniverse
1663 Liberty Drive
Bloomington, IN 47403
www.iuniverse.com
1-800-Authors (1-800-288-4677)

ISBN: 978-1-4502-6192-0 (pbk)
ISBN: 978-1-4502-6191-3 (ebk)

Printed in the United States of America

iUniverse rev. date: 10/2/12

Contents

Author with sister Sarah: Victory Garden veggies from Long Island country place in 1943, and on the left with gleaned greens from Great Oak Farm, Berlin, Mass., November, 2008!

Introduction

In this day of the revival of interest in gardening and local organic farms, I thought a
farm Journal from the heady days of the Back to the Earth movement and experiments
with communal enterprise and equality of gender, would be of general interest. I
kept a diary or journal over the farm season of 1972 (May through October) at Willet
Produce Farm, a communal organic farm located in central New York State 25 miles
south of Cortland. In the back of the Journal written 6 months later are descriptions
of visits to the farm in August and November and December, 1971. Jarlath Hamrock,
who never left Willet, kept the Journal in the farm bookcase and gave it back to me a
few years ago. I transcribed the Journal and tracked down the other farm partners
for their recollections. We all gathered for a 36th year reunion over Labor Day 2008.
Interestingly the catalyst for our gathering and my contacting my former farm partners
was a phone call I received from a celebrity reporter trying to find out about Yoko Ono's
reported sojourn at a farm neighbor's place to rest during her pregnancy! It must have
occurred after our time there for no one had any memory of it, but it got us all talking
to one another and lead to our reunion and this book!

I asked Dan Keller to write a short introduction. Dan still lives and farms at the
communal farm everyone called Wendell Farm, which is described in the Journal. His
occupation is filming documentaries such as *Peace Trip, Vietnam: the Secret Agent,
Cannabis Rising, Lovejoy's Nuclear War.* His company is Green Mountain Post Films.
Dan is a 1969 graduate of Amherst College, part of the anti-Vietnam War and anti-
nuclear generation. Dan Keller:

> These days when we say "the Sixties" we mean the infamous decade of
> the 1960's, which saw the explosion of the anti-war movement (the Vietnam
> war,) the civil rights movement, the women's movement, the black power
> movement, the flower power movement, and, often overshadowed by these
> momentous changes, the back to the land movement.

This was a wave of mostly youngsters who left the cities and populated small towns from Maine to California, with the belief that there is something good and important about growing food, living off the land, and respecting mother earth. Often when one of these old farms was "liberated," another would soon appear down the road, and then another in the next town, and these farms would be connected by sharing farm equipment, bartering, or intermarriage, although the actual ritual of marriage was not practiced. Work was hard and life was often tough for these folks, but there was a healthy amount of entertainment, especially rock and roll and everything associated with it. Generally speaking, the vegetables and fruits that were being grown were organic, that is produced without chemical fertilizers or pesticides, thus adding substantial energy to the organic food movement. Robert Rodale, the editor of Organic Gardening Magazine, called the back to the landers "America's New Peasantry."

The movement continues today. Many of the farms are still alive, and over the last few decades a steady supply of young people have been populating small and large farms around the world. This journal captures much of the spirit of appreciation for nature that was the cornerstone of the back to the land movement. It is also a powerful evocation of the rambunctious, ebullient, idealistic, and explosive energy of the times.

It is now December 2010, 38 years after the prime years of Willet Produce Farm! Preceding the transcription of my Journal, I have described my personal background and some of the events leading up to my moving out to the farm that year, including a Journal description of my first visits there the year before (August, November and December 1971). Then I asked the farm founders and partners and other visitors to contribute their recollections, as well as summarizing their subsequent lives. The post 1972 years at Willet are mostly described by Jarlath Hamrock, the present owner. I write about my own subsequent life. The book concludes with the telling of the farm reunion weekend Labor Day, 2008.

First I have reprinted extensive quotes from an article about Willet Produce Farm by Mark Kramer which inspired my participation! It had the arresting title of *Chicken Shit People* and was published in July, 1971, in an alternative newspaper the *Boston Phoenix*, later to be published as a chapter in a book. Clabberville is Colrain in the hill country of western Massachusetts, and Willet is in central New York State about 25 miles south and east of Cortland, N.Y.

[For reasons of privacy some people's names were altered, and a word or two changed. O.P.]

Chicken Shit People

Chapter in *Mother Walter & the Pig Tragedy* by
Mark Kramer, Alfred A. Knopf, 1972

. . . It's not hard to find the effects of the standardization and concentration of food growing right here in Clabberville. There's a roadside stand set up by an old farmer named Bishop Stewart which offers plum tomatoes, four or five breeds of regular tomatoes, and yellow pear-shaped tomatoes as well. Last year, for the first time, Bishop had to take part of his harvest down to the wholesale vegetable market near Springfield and sell it in competition with the regular growers. He got no premium for variety—in fact he couldn't move the yellow ones—no premium for his craft, and he barely broke even on his summer's tomato harvest. The following summer he put in half his usual crop, just what he could move at the stand to old customers and no more, and who's to blame him?

All this explanation is just to set the stage for the extraordinary enterprise of the chicken shit people. The chicken shit people are five men and one woman who have started up a three-hundred-acre organic farm in central New York State *(Willet, N.Y.)*. The magnitude of that ambition is astounding.

Jim and George and Ira have all farmed before. They were part of the largest commercial organic farm I know about around here—raising about a dozen acres of corn, melons, potatoes, and a few other vegetables on a cooperative basis. They made enough to live on, working long hours and depending on their numbers (about ten) to make up for their shortage of specialized machinery, a practice not open to straight farmers because of high labor costs. That farm is still going on, but Jim and George and Ira have all left for the big time.

"I've traveled all over," said George, "lived in a lot of different scenes (he once taught English in Saudi Arabia) and whatever I do, I keep coming back to farming because it makes me happy." Ira is a beefy, whip-smart Jewish kid who still has some incompletes at Amherst, and who has in the past few years taught himself to build houses and rebuild old truck engines because Amherst wouldn't teach him those things.

And Jim, at twenty-three, has earned the respectful nickname of Doc—he says, "It won't stick, but it's nice"—because when machines break he keeps smiling and soon has them back in operation. He is a master welder with a flair for improvised repairs that keep working, and the energy to keep hard at a job as long as there's light to see. George has brought in his friends Caesar and Dick, both young students in agriculture school. Caesar's mother kept an organic garden for years ("She never called it that, but it was") and this gave him the hint that the ag school fertilizer-pesticide-herbicide method might not be the only True Way.

Jim bought an old gravel dump truck for $750—the kind you see on heavy road-building projects—which had been retired from road-building and then retired from a long subsequent career with a local contractor. He "got it running good again"—a phrase that smooths over weeks of anguish and dirty work—and set out for the new farm with Linda, who had put an ad in Organic Gardening asking for a summer job on a farm. She got more than she bargained for, and is now a member in good standing of the new enterprise.

Central New York State is real big-time farm country. Having just come back from there, I wonder all the more at the stubborn New Englanders who continue to work their three acres of corn on the side of some hill, and seven acres of good hay won from the little shoulder of bottomland above the river. These New York farms have single fields of forty and fifty acres of beautiful rolling land, and on the dairy farms, herds of several hundred milkers are not uncommon.

After months of searching, the five men had located an abandoned place high up a dirt road, with poor barns falling in, a poor house, salvageable, but it's cold in the winter, and two hundred acres of lovely tillable open land rolling across three hills, nearly one hundred acres of pasture, and about fifty acres of woodlot. They got it for about a third the asking price of a working farm.

Next they found an old chicken farm nearby, and for the price of a beer down at the Brown Beaver, the old man who used to work it let them have a veritable treasure in chicken shit. So George's old Farmall H, and an old M that came with the farm, and Jim's wonderful 1935 John Deere A, a two-cylinder job with external flywheel and hand clutch, trundled in a brigade down to the chicken farm, followed by the resurrected dump truck. They scraped and loaded ton after ton of chicken shit, rumbled home again an again through the crossroads of bar, gas station, post office, and general store, called the center of town, and won their name: the Chicken Shit People.

At first the local bloods griped about the disservice those longhairs (not Jim—he's the resident townie) were perpetrating, bringing that nasty ammonia smell into town, and talked about dumping a load on the front steps of the farmhouse some night. Soon they were drinking and playing pool with our heroes, and not long after that were coming up and lending a hand haying or helping to put together a "new" wagon. Willet Produce is the first new scene in town since tractors came into style, and it has not been long in gaining a welcome.

The local equipment dealer came up and offered them the opportunity to try out a mammoth tractor with wheels higher than a man stands, which pulls four plows at once through the toughest sod. It got a sore test right away. Dick seized the opportunity to turn over thirty acres of old acid sod, dense with orchard grass, strawberries, blackberries, and buttercups in the low spots—a field nearly a mile and a half in perimeter.

Five of us went out, paced off a centerline at different points across the field and stood in the tall grass marking each spot as the tractor lugged down the line. At dusk the tractor finally roared up to the house. Dick grabbed some supper while Caesar and Clem from town raided the junk-car lot in back of the barn, came back with two sealed-beam headlamps, and roped and wired them into place. Then it was back to the field. At dawn I was awakened by the sound of their return from work. Two others took their place, and by noon the next day, the field was done, ready for harrowing and the sowing of buckwheat. Then Linda drove the tractor back down to the equipment dealer and thanked him for the "free home trial. "

The seed was combined late in September. It commanded a premium price and helped pay for a new tractor they can use at a slower pace. The buckwheat also served as an effective "smother" crop. It is a prolific spreader and does well in spent soil. It's a frost-sensitive annual, and if the seed is collected, one is left a clear field of stubble in spring, suitable for planting to corn or good mowing.

They also sowed winter wheat and put in several acres of melons and feed corn, some other vegetables, have taken twenty acres of hay, and set out a king-sized house garden. It seems a miracle, but the new farm is underway—one of the first eastern efforts to supply the demand for new health foods, grown as small private growers used to grow them before the age of standard quality. Their life-style and handiness have allowed them to do it on nearly no money, save what they borrowed from friends and fathers as down payment on the farm.

But it is rare. Few farmers understand the peculiar marketing practices necessary to make a go selling to consumers of organic food. And few freaks understand the ways of farming well enough to do the job. Of those who do, fewer still want to work that hard. I think it will be a long time before enterprises like Willet Produce are common enough to lower the premium prices of natural foods, prices now determined by the need to import grain from Texas, meat from Arkansas, and vegetables from California.

Note: The article concluded with a plea for people to invest in the Willet Produce enterprise!

How Author ended up at Willet

Personal Background

During the fall of 1971, I was a little restless working for the Conservation Law Foundation. Law, even if for a good cause, was not my thing! With Freddie, the young woman who worked for me as secretary, we sent out letters to quite a few foundations, Letters of Inquiry, as is the word of art. Only about half the foundations answered, and they all answered in the negative, that they were not interested in receiving a grant proposal from us.

Then I had cooked up an annual meeting featuring one Victor Yanaccone, one of the founders of the Environmental Defense Fund, who promoted a constitutional right to a clean environment based on the 9th Amendment. In truth a far out claim, but he was of interest, one of the first to bring a lawsuit versus the use of DDT. But the CLF President took a conservative view and over my head cancelled the event!

I inherited some stock around that time, and the Back to the Earth movement was in full swing. There was a lot of talk of organic farming, and it reminded me of the pleasures of living in the country and working in my mother's Victory Garden as a child. We lived on Long Island—West Hills, Huntington—in the summers, also spring and fall weekends. Our garden was big, close to an acre; that's my sister Sarah posing with me in the intro' photo. We also raised Barred Rock chickens for their eggs, and turkeys for T-Day. We had a 16 acre meadow in front of our house, planted in corn two or three of the war years by a neighbor farmer. I could ride my brother's ex polo pony Hi Ho through the woods and bicycle six miles to the Beach Club in Cold Spring Harbor where we played tennis and sailed. Gas was rationed. I was 8 almost 9 Pearl Harbor day, coincidentally my father's birthday! He was 41, too old for the draft. . .

Back to the present — well — 1971. In the back of my Journal (written a year later) I describe the correspondence with Mark Kramer, the offer to invest in the farm, and what happened—meeting the farm partners and journeying out to the farm, my first impressions!

Journal — August 1971

So — last year — Mark Kramer, who writes the column 'Living in the Country' for the Boston Phoenix asked in one of his columns for correspondence, and I wrote him a letter in which I said I was interested in investing in an organic farm (tho' if I remember it right, I didn't say I was interested in large-scale farming, rather something small scale). Anyway, he wrote me about Willet, enclosing his hype article about it, and not more than maybe 10 days or two weeks later Caesar, Ira and Jim show up at the Conservation Law Foundation in their farming togs for sure with great smiles and much hair and I'm amazed! We all hit it off! I take them to Sanae *[a macrobiotic restaurant]* where we all feast on the buffet, and then we walk down to Erewhon's *[an organic grocery store]*, the three of them all ogling the girls on the street and behaving in general like country hicks!

Ira describes my father and uncle at Amherst (he went to Amherst College as I did) *[my father was a Trustee and my uncle the President, George Jacobs, a farm partner, was class of 1968, Ira 1969, myself 1954!]*. My father and uncle were in their three-piece suits as though to pass judgment on all the long-haired, raggedly dressed students, *[my father and uncle facing the assembled students protesting the Vietnam War!]*.

Anyway they say I can't invest in the farm unless I spend some time on the farm and work on it, so it is left that I'll come out in a while, and I gave Ira $150 *[as earnest money — as I remember it I ended up investing $5,000, receiving stock in return, as the farm had been organized as a corporation to facilitate changes in ownership by a lawyer uncle]*. Among other nice signs they are all driving a SAAB *[I owned a SAAB at the time]*.

They wanted me to come out almost immediately, but naturally I don't get it up to go for a while, until some two weeks later I get a phone call from Mary Beth, or Chica as is her nick-name, who is in Boston to see someone who turns out not to be there (in a hospital), and she needs a ride back to Willet. So I decide to set forth for Willet giving her a ride — this is around August 10th or so.

Arrive late at night — people still up drinking wine and talking loudly, all these people sleeping in the next room — all most satisfactory in some way — earthy for sure, like Mexico, this Appalachian shack! A woman named Linda takes me to find a place to sleep in one of the farm barns.

The next morning Ira gives me the tour — the fields, rows of vegetables, the woods. Everyone is working on this barn a couple of miles away on a job to raise money for the farm, so I work with Ira on some pinning up of the first floor on this part of the barn, while others are on top putting on roof boards, and of course to get there we all drive like mad! Of the three weeks I stay we work off and on on the barn for much of the time — perhaps two or three times as long as they all predict, various difficulties arising. The last part, putting on tar paper, quite a trip, everyone falling down at least once, getting all tarred up!

Otherwise our routine every day — as I remember it seemed every day was a perfect hot day, getting up early with fog in the valleys — the day starting out by picking blackberries in the woods! We got fearsome scratches from the thorns! Truly prolific, great big berries; we also picked in the meadows — smaller berries but even more prolific!

Then the veggies — green beans, peas, corn, thinning carrots, all for the daily run to the stand in Cortland, and occasionally for freezing — I remember one morning shelling peas. Linda and Chica run the kitchen, baking bread for the stand, Linda taking me along one day to get milk and chat with a farmer across the valley, Chica taking me blueberry picking to this wild blueberry pasture nearby (several miles).

Lets see, what else — Keller comes from Wendell — we go to get chicken shit. Ira shows me how to work the John Deere, and I pull boards across this field *[part of the field prep]*. We have amazing day picking corn for Cortland State University — contract for 3,000 shucked ears — meaning like Ira and I picked all one afternoon — it was hot so I took my clothes off (!) like freedom, right? Then the next morning most of us, maybe 8 of us, picked and shucked corn all morning to make it! Then we had to deliver it to Cortland, all for 4 ¢ an ear — $120 — all to be eaten in one course for lunch!

Weekends were something else — all this drinking and girls at the Beaver, like being back in college! I don't know — for all its disadvantages attracted me over the civilization of the city, it seemed to be the place. Like after listening to Ralph Nader once, it made me feel hot with anger, and want to throw nails on the Southeast Expressway and rebel altogether, drop out, but somehow the negativity of that depressed me. This way there is something positive to relate to, like having a beautiful garden — but to become a central New York organic farmer??

Brookline Street, Cambridge

After my three weeks at Willet I returned to Cambridge where I lived at the time, to my apartment in a 9 apartment triple-decker on Brookline Street near the Charles River which friends of mine had persuaded me to invest in! It was going to be just an investment, the concept to starting rehab a decaying urban building in the path of the 'Inner Belt' which Governor Sargent had just rescued by canceling. But the tenants had objected to my agent's raising the rent before rehab starting, and when I met all of them, long hair and late rising, I took their side and fired my agent! Then when one of the three room apartments became vacant I moved in. One of the tenants became my 'crew chief' to rehab all the windows. He recommended rebuilding all the frames instead of just putting in new windows, so we embarked on a more serious rehab than had been planned. Most of this occurred just after my summer at Willet. Later in time (1973) a number of tenants came out to Willet, and one who stayed there off and on, Jarlath Hamrock, became Willet's owner and remains so today (2009)!

The Brookline Street gang sitting across the street, and the building itself 1974!

BORDERLAND

For some reason I did not record the 'Borderland raid' in my Journal, taking place September, 1971. Borderland had been my grandparent's place in North Easton, Mass., 1,250 acres of woods and fields and ponds with three farmhouses and a stone mansion; in December, 1970, it became a State park—google Borderland State Park! I became quite involved in the process, leading an introductory walk the spring of 1971, and helping to form a Friends of Borderland organization. In fact I was its first president. At the time parks personnel were foresters, unused to the idea of park interpretation, and definitely not up on managing a house museum which this was, the family having donated the antique furnishings and my grandmother's art (portraits and landscapes, botanical drawings, etc.) — also there was a two story library. The Friends organized house tours, nature walks, concerts and the like. Fortunately the second supervisor was trained in more up-to-date park management and was simpatico with the Friends' ideas.

Meanwhile, back then, one day, I asked the supervisor whether the 1954 Ford tractor he had inherited from my grandmother was useful. He replied, "not especially." This was just after I had returned from Willet, the fall of 1971. I communicated same to my new-found partners out at Willet. They immediately proposed they come and liberate said tractor. It had a front-end loader which the other farm tractors lacked. I conferred with my grandmother's superintendent who had stayed on with the State (he lived in one of the farm houses and was payed a small pension). We arranged for the transfer of the tractor on a weekend the State supervisor was absent. They drove out all the way from Willet, some 7 hours away with a huge truck. With difficulty we drove the Ford up boards into the truck. We also loaded the Model A jalopy my grandmother had fixed up with my mechanical brother back when (my grandmother was good at mechanics). It had just two bucket seats in front and a platform in back, no fenders, doors, roof, etc. We drove it madly around the cart roads of Borderland starting at (my) age 13 or so!

There was small Hell to pay for that act of what you might view as a theft! I had to write contrite letters and resign from being Friends' president! Then I further roiled the waters by throwing a kind of good-bye party the first weekend of October out at Borderland, unfortunately choosing the same weekend as a Willet organized Oktoberfest!

Mansion at Borderland

9

Borderland Party — Willet Oktoberfest

That fall, I thought to organize a good-bye party out at Borderland! I invited all my Cambridge newfound new generation friends (some were hippies), and all the farm folk I knew, from Wendell Commune, Montague Commune, and Packers Corners in southern Vermont where lived Veronica Porche, and Raymond Mungo. Ray wrote a book about that farm called *Total Loss Farm!* Unfortunately George Jacobs et al at Willet had organized an Oktoberfest the same weekend! Ah well! So people from Willet and Wendell and Montague didn't come, with the exception of Jarlath, who was still really a Cambridge person.

It was an amazing party, seemingly all 1000 acres of Borderland thronged with people. The Packers Corner crowd came dressed in Victorian costume and decorously walked around carrying sun umbrellas! I took everyone out on the Jalopy. Then I gave Ace the "keys" (no keys of course) and he drove people around. I gave house tours, showing off my grandparent's awesome two-story library, all their turn-of-the-century furniture and paintings (most by my grandmother). By coincidence my first cousin Ned Ames was there with his wife Suzie and their kids. At one point she was playing a Victorian dance for the kids on the piano in the living room while Verandah and an English girl Joan were doing a great dance around the front hall. Outside I spent a peaceful moment watching two Tree Frog kids play tennis. . .

In the middle of all this I spied a blond crew cut man approach the house. I leaned out the window and called, "Who are you?" The man replied with the same phrase, "And who are you??" It was my 1st cousin Ollie, who like his father, my Uncle Ollie, was not enamored as I was with the hippie revolution! I had grown a beard, so I definitely wasn't recognizable by Ollie. Fortunately my cousin Ned, whom I knew better, closer to my age, mediated. My aunt from Nashville called, upset over the fact there were people's dogs in the house. My cousin had told his father, who then called my aunt in Tennessee. I was surprised, for my aunt was a real dog person — they raised Irish setters, also toy poodles, which were transported up to Borderland to roam the fields and keep my grandmother company. But of course your own dog is not the same as someone else's dog!

Perhaps the day was capped by our swimming nude at Puds Pond. It just happened a local man was out there fishing (local people had the permission to fish the ponds). So, right away the whole town of Easton knew we were swimming naked at Puds Pond, Borderland!

In the mean time, Oktoberfest out at Willet was apparently quite a party, people from Wendell and Montague there, all the town there — three days of revelry!! They had a great barn fire, roasted a pig, and the Wendell band played under a full moon, a beautiful night. . .

Winter at Willet

Written a year later, end of the Journal, visits taking place in November & December, 1971.

Came out to Willet around Thanksgiving, and saw winter arrive literally — no freeze up to that time, like played volleyball one day in 65 or 70 degrees weather, then snow squall the next day — a great cold wind shudders the house!

Also came out for a week after Christmas. We played pool at brother George's on the way up — Ira, Jim Aaron, Dick Bogden and all the Plimpton cousins were there — Teddy, David, Polly, Nat.

Willet was beautiful in the snow and cold for sure! Dick gives George *[Jacobs]* the needle to do stuff — "Come on big Daddy!" By this time the farm has a cow as well as chickens and ducks, also a pig, and at night they would all sleep together for warmth — for all a manger scene!

The next day we actually go out to harvest feed corn in the snow, the yellow of the kernels contrasting with the white and pale yellow of the snow and stalks. Then a great winter sunset — pale, subtle pinks and greens and greys!

We all go out one day to cut down this huge cherry tree, maybe 90 feet high or more. Night fell before we could finish cutting it down, but a great wind storm arose at night, so when we went out the next morning, the great tree had fallen, practically felling two maples with it. We had a terrific time trying to pull the logs out from the woods, getting constantly stuck; in fact we had to wait for some special equipment the next day to get it out — all this for John Anderson who crafts guitars, the wood having to age for five years. We took the logs to a mill, and they were cut into boards and then stored in the barn. . .

As I remember it, I spent most of the winter working at the Conservation Law Foundation and on my Cambridgeport building, but come Spring, around the 1st of May, I set forth for Willet!

Winter at Willet — horse barn (now gone), barn and the house.

Willet Journal

— 1972 —

<u>May 16, 1972</u>: Looks like I'll actually write in this book! Am in Willet — an organic
farm in central New York State, as one can see from the dirt on this page. Crazy that
I'm here! Had "good bye" party in Cambridge in my apartment Saturday night. Sunday
we planted forsythia bushes in front yard — afternoon took off for Wendell *[Commune]*
— place really looks like my dream of a rural place — earthy — in a valley with stream
rushing by — reminded me of Indian village in Mexico — rainy warm weather. Sunday
went by Mark Kramer's place *[Colrain]* to pick up some tools. Drove out to Willet —
too lonely and long. Picked up some hitchhikers, who I got to like, from Toronto (no,
London) Ontario. He was giving girl friend (and me) whole rap about astrology — how
being Pisces she didn't say what was in her head or let out her feelings. I told about my
ex girl friend being emotional — wasn't that typical Pisces? But no, rather yes he said—
Pisces divided. Struck me whole thing kind of a metaphor — in the way of giving more
weight to one's basic nature (genetics) versus psychiatric (environment). Wanted to
hold hands with the girl — she was sitting in front, but didn't. Maybe it'd be better off if
I did more often what I want to do! He described trip on bicycle (up to 125 miles a day),
and the friendly generous people who took him in; we agreed he couldn't do it again
both personally and because of increased suspicion and paranoia out there generally.

Got here about 5:00 p.m. — Ira, George, Jill, Claire and Hamish — an agricultural
student from Scotland. Promptly ate some goodies Ira brought from New York. Have
made and hereby make resolution to quite eating so much — yuk. Am getting fat
besides.

Went to agricultural meeting with Jerry, someone from Cornell and the women.
Town looks just like Iowa. Went to Jerry's after—played pool and drank beer. George
and Jill really swill it down. Jerry talks about being a beatnik in the Village. Told
them one of the reasons I'm out here is that Ira, George, Keller, Sam and others from
Amherst (College) really told off my Uncle and Father, which I've never had whatever it
is to do directly. This place reminds me of the Army; got out some of my army clothes
when went by Long Island, but they depress me. Remember to write about first week

here as long as am writing this. *[Apparently didn't enter first week's events, also page torn and hard to read]*

Thunderstorm outside. Just saw a Blue-gray Gnatcatcher in bush outside. Slept in the barn last night — couldn't see so woke up in a pile of cow shit (which was OK). A nice trilling frog is outside house where septic tank flows over.

Today (morning) transplanted (that's ahead) rather put soil in pea pots for melon planting in the greenhouse. Difficult to see how I can really relate to this place, because it is not an equal venture — I don't feel like an equal partner — my knowledge and experience is too different from theirs. Like it really does remind me of being in the Army — like the pool playing, beer drinking, my acting my funny part — no, more really of Amherst, also of Iowa and the summer spent working on the pipe line in British Columbia. Amherst, Army, British Columbia have in common that I am flunky, joker, slave type, etc. without any control of my destiny. Think I'll stick it out, though if some really good opportunity comes along may split.

May 17, Tuesday: Jerry came over tonight — long discussion, partly about use of words "nigger" and "cunt". Ira says nigger in the way of poking fun at liberals. Claire uptight about use of cunt — derogatory.

Pretty nice day — walked up on the hill — saw Redstarts, Chestnut-sided Warbler, Bobolinks yet — flying up in the air and singing all the way down.

Transplanted some lettuce. Went to town with Ira to get plumbing supplies, not much work. Eggs for breakfast, egg salad for lunch, lentil soup for supper. What else — Ira is comparing us to Russian intellectuals being banned to Siberia — we're like that! Cultural desert!

About last week when I was here saw great 7s of geese flying across the sky, and watched deer close leap and re-leap a fence — their tails really big white flags. Also saw bluebirds. Like place is beautiful — nice sunset tonight — rain falling here and there in the distance.

May 18, Wednesday — we don't get up so early, around 9:00 — breakfast of eggs and home-made bread (toast). Went out to take a shit which did in woodchuck hole — looked abandoned, hope so for w.c.'s sake. Surprised some deer in the woods — one of them snorted and you could see all their tails go up.

Ira spent whole day fixing the plumbing down in the basement. George and Jill spend all their time driving around wheeling dealing, though George finds a little time here and there to pull the brush cutter through the corn stalks, make flats, this and that which he does very efficiently. A lot of repair work on the tractor heisted from Borderland.

Saw Great Blue Heron flying across the sky — usual nice sunset. We all had long talk about our situations, relationships to families, etc.

May 19, Thursday: Another really nice summer-like day — more transplanting, made flats. Most of afternoon spent trying to extract dump truck with load of bull shit (I mean chicken shit) — power wagon (truck), Super C and Ford — everything in turn got stuck. Finally Jerry, who was behind all this (his chicken shit) called up some friend with a Caterpillar, who, with much further effort (after load dumped) finally pulled us out, though this will cost some. — Went down to hear the frog chorus — they stop altogether, then start up as a movement in a symphony.

May 20, — Somehow dates are mixed up as today is Saturday (now Sunday). Rainy day — weather man had said zero chance of rain — we had been watching news — Vietnam, Wallace. Spent most of the day transplanting, in fact re-transplanting as we had followed directions twice the thickness of the seed, meaning really shallow, while turns out it should be four times the breadth or width or about ¾ inch. Went for a few misty walks — trees really nice colors. Collected some flowers, and oh yeh, made some peanut muffins and my very first bread — whole wheat — and even made pancakes for breakfast and macaroni casserole (peppers, mushrooms, cheese and tomatoes) and spinach for supper, and washed everything in addition! Girls like me (Claire). People come by from N. J. who are starting a farm nearby. We all watch Miss U.S.A. George puts some drag clothes on! Wrote a long letter to [brother] George.

May 21, Sunday: Got up at 7:30, fog, went for walk — trilliums in the woods — saw a duck fly out of a tree — must have been a wood duck. Made Ralston cereal for breakfast. More transplanting. Sun comes out — beautiful day. Go for walk with Claire. Watch a hawk play tag with a barn swallow, that while lazing in the sun. Really nice in the woods — purple trillium, bleeding hearts (?) (an intricate delicate white flower). Cool our feet in a stream. Smell of hay amazing. Blossoms too.

Go with George and Ira to get chicken shit. First have to extract stuck dump truck at Jerry's, pulling it out with the power wagon. Must have had the trucks going full tilt for 15 minutes rocking before it came out. At chicken shit pile, drove the tractor (family's) to load. Ira kept getting stuck, but we made a better path into it. This is a great molten pile left after the chicken house burned down. Managed to get the knack of it charging in getting a load in the front end loader, and then dumping that into the dump truck. With an enormous load we proceeded down this quite steep hill in first (brakes shaky). Then on the way up the driveway hill, Ira goofed, and the front end of the truck somehow went up into the air some 5 feet! And we started rolling back towards the ditch, me fumbling with the door handle! [Ira succeeded in righting it!]. Then we got stuck again, and broke the headlight in the process of pulling out. Adventuresome these huge machines!

Nice sunset. Played a little soccer with Ira. People talk of building shelters tomorrow.

May 22, Monday — everyone got up real early (6 a.m.) to look for shelters, led by Ira, George off to get chicken shit. Found a really suitable maple for Jill to use for tree house. Again a beautiful day — didn't do too much, sat around in the sun. Only got into plowing towards the end. Satisfying job that, sitting endlessly on the machine watching the sun go down, and the birds coming to pick at the insects aroused.

May 23, Tuesday—Like 6 a.m. again. Went over to get Ford tractor left at chicken farm, it decided we have enough. Rig holding cans of stone on back had broken — things are always breaking out here, or are out of repair to start with. George and Ira are geniuses at fixing things, the rest of us out of it concerning all this equipment.

Girls (Claire, Jill, Dianne—friend of Jill's newly arrived) get together to demand more participation in the goings on at the farm, and fairer distribution of kitchen duties, so that they get to drive the tractors. This leads to George cooking dinner (good)! And my showing both Claire and Jill how to drive the John Deere with plow (blind leading the blind)! Spent most of the day on tractor plowing. Took breaks for various reasons, one to call mother and George to try and raise some money, as we're really broke. Got 500 from mother.

Had tough time starting John Deere (you have to pull around a kind of wheel) after it had run out of gas. At the end of the day took John Deere on tour of the farm, up to the top of the hill, Jill driving! Took bath.

JOURNAL POEM ABOUT PLOWING A FIELD WITH THE JOHN DEERE

Wrote poem in my Journal, altered slightly on April 18th, 2008. To say a little more about the John Deere tractor, I believe it was a 1938 model. The wheel in question is about two feet in diameter, located on the side. You could grasp it with two hands and give it a spin — a little similar to the starting devise on old cars where you spun a handle around. It took some energy to spin this wheel — perhaps you could spin it around a dozen times in a minute. You could keep at it as long as ten minutes sometimes to get it started, maybe even longer, resting in between efforts! Once you get the tractor started, its motor rhythm is quite slow and loud. The engine has only two cylinders, but they are large. The noise of the tractor reverberates across the valley, but it is not a bothersome noise really; you get used to it. . .

ODE TO PLOWING

The plow turns the soil just so — neat — so that the turf is exactly turned over;
The chugging John Deere pulls the plow along at a measured pace—a slow walk,
So you have a long time to sit, or rather stand as I do —
You really get to know the field and the trees around,
Especially the sky above and the sun,
And the view of the hills, for the farm is on a hill.

You watch the birds that come for the insects disturbed
By the turning over of the sod — the brown and black of the Cowbird,
Olive green of the female, the sheen of the Grackle, red of the Redwing,
Occasionally a Killdeer, or a Crow comes by;
The crow will fly to the opposite end of the field from you.

I take my clothes off and ride the tractor naked.
No one there to see me, I am all alone out there.
It takes from about 10 to 2 and 3 to 9 to plow the field!
Occasionally you have to mind the tractor,
Braking one wheel when the front wheel gets caught in a rut,
Steering of course, then getting off to move a boulder.

The field curves just so you can't see the farmhouse and barns,
And then you see the roofs emerge as a Wyeth painting.
I daydream of various things I would like to do with my life.
And watch the sun set in slowest motion.

PHOTOS PASTED IN THE FARM JOURNAL

THE HOUSE

The View with Fog and After it Lifts

Kitchen—Dan Bogdan, Ceasar, George Sherman; August 1971—Oakes, Goon, Dan, Chica

George Jacobs weeding by horsebarn; Ice Cream at Cincinnatus: Wendy/Lyn/Claire/Dana!

End of May — June!

<u>Wednesday, May 24</u>: Dreamt people read this Journal. Up not so early — went over to help Alexa by spreading chicken shit on their garden. Plowed most of the day.

Claire is sick — has blood clots from her period which is a miscarriage. Jill and Diane take her to hospital to have minor operation to complete the miscarriage — she's OK now.

Not a good day — Ford springs an oil leak, water goes out, power take off goes on Dodge powerwagon, which we thought could pull the manure spreader. Ira and George now trying to fix these things. At 10 p.m. can hear someone plowing — unlike us they have lights on their tractor.

<u>Thursday, May 25</u>: Having stalled the John Deere, spent much pain getting it started again. Lots of time spent hitching up equipment. Drove the manure spreader behind the John Deere, the flailing chains spreading the chicken shit, some of it flying into my hair, still picking it out of my hair at supper (tho' dry by then).

Claire back and healthy, recovered from operation! Cooked us a dinner of Chinese fried rice (ingredients including mushrooms, broccoli, onions, etc.). Burlap, her dog, lost without her — led me on a walk up to the top of the hill last night. Long talk going on downstairs on the enigma that is Ira! Wrote Gerry and Kaysie, and Kelly for loans *[Boston friends]*.

<u>Friday, May 26</u>—this being Saturday night — just came back from ice cream place in Cincinnatus *[neighboring town]*. Visited Jerry's place but no one there. Full moon tonight! Last night out there these seed potatoes arrived in a truly huge truck, and we unloaded 100 100 pound bags — a huge pile of potatoes — to plant 5 acres. An acre of potatoes will yield from 20 to 30 tons! Somehow I guess we're going to get the equipment to deal with it (some $400 worth). George thinks there is a big market for organic potatoes.

After loading potatoes we're sitting here, Ira reading me Yeats and Blake (the latter amazing), when Jill yells out, "fire in the greenhouse!" We all tear out of the house expecting the worse, but its kerosene leaked from the 'salamander' *[name for the heater]* ablaze on the floor. It wasn't too hard to put it out.

Has been really beautiful these last few days, especially yesterday — almost a fall day in clarity — all the apple blossoms out in force. Been taking walks with Burlap, Claire's dog in the early a.m. and p.m. Lets see, in the last two days (well today), spread phosphate and ran the manure spreader later on (got George with it, it really throws out the shit!). Yesterday also spread phosphate. Taught Jill how to run the plow, and started a field. To bed...

Saturday, May 27: Another cloudless beautiful clear day! Plowed first thing up in the feed corn field. Wrote some letters — much sitting around — we run out of gas in the tanks, so blow mind of local store by filling tank (or rather putting in) 73.4 gallons of gas—$30 worth, the tank having been put on the Dodge power wagon by the front end loader of the Ford. Went swimming nude in the river — really nice — the four of us including Dana who just arrived, who went to school with Jim Ord. Jim came up later to bitch about his situation, asking for his money back, etc. *[Jim Ord was a founding partner as mentioned in Mark Kramer's article; see his story following the Journal transcription. Dick Bogdan and Jim Lesser (Caesar), also featured, were just graduated from Agricultural School and they moved on to other endeavors.]*

Jerry comes by with one of his "mail order" girls. He has all these people removing rocks from his garden. *[Apologies to Jerry, who subsequently wrote me that 'the girls' were women from the New Jersey Yoga Institute, who were staying at his house for a weekend retreat.]* Argument at dinner between George and Jill and Ira over Jerry. Ira's been in a bad mood lately — too much communal living (and maybe too much responsibility). We made arrangements to plow all night, by the moon, but the Ford is too difficult to handle.

Monday and Tuesday, May 28, 29: Its Tuesday and raining at last. Thunder. I was really disagreeable this morning and argumentative, and angry with George for his blithe disregard of reality! Plowed some at night on two huge fields with the Ford. Real bitch, for the wheels keep spinning, and one would have to keep adjusting the plow. OK in the morning with wild mustard to look at, and the greening of the trees — the buckwheat field, and this one near the house — some 5 or 600 yards, a half an hour practically to do one turn! The moon came out, and did one turn under its light, but no good. Bitched to George, so we (mainly George) made this arrangement to weight the back end of the tractor with a box full of heavy metal things, but it broke up almost immediately, so that this junk iron was left in the middle of the field... More plowing, etc.

This incredible old man wanders up the hill and carries on. Jill gets along well with him, which reminds me that the other day was sitting in the outhouse when Jill demonstrated its two-holeness by saying she couldn't wait, and sat down beside me, which seemed altogether natural. Had adventure with Jill today which was that she got the John Deere stuck all the way up to its hub caps practically in a mud hole. Drove up with the 'power wagon' (Ira's ancient Dodge truck) and almost got that stuck. Pulled away the plow by dint of some 25 feet of chain, and then amazingly got the tractor out on its own. When we went to hitch up the hydraulics of the plow, forgot the power take off being on and the oil spewed forth from the hole squirting all over me! Had on short shorts (cut off blue jeans from junk pile of clothes). Took mud bath to try and what-do-you-call-it — neutralize it. We all got to laughing with Jill driving the power wagon, as it took to lurching as hiccups (speeding up and slowing down).

The other happening today was the running out of gas. The great truck came, and almost ran into him [the old man] coming off the field. Then ran out of gas in the Ford while taking the tank off the power wagon; had to put some in from the tank he had just filled, and in addition we couldn't move the power wagon as it was out of gas!

People talking downstairs — went down to see what's up — nice rain outside. Made pumpkin pie for supper! Good — made big mistake which was to treat the frozen pumpkin filling as though it was just pumpkin, but still good. Made two pies hence.

Got 1,000 dollars for the farm today. Took some of the pressure off me. Been trying to ferret some money out of [brother] George — difficult to get in touch with him.

Wednesday, May 30: RAIN — good part of the day. Drove to New Hope Mills to see water driven mill and buy flour — beautiful lake — mill most satisfactory. Once there were 15 mills along the stream, now all gone save one — sad!

New guy has arrived from N.J. to learn about farming, through Rodale. We spent most of the afternoon building a stand for the sink in bathroom, which we solved by finding stuff already made, and hooking it up. Split pea soup and cornbread for dinner, by Claire.

Thursday, May 31: More rain—dreary. We all went to Cincinnatus to have coffee, donuts and French fries. Worked more on the sink. No water again, and we run out of gas. Ira leaves with Bill, Ira for the dentist — 1st time in 8 years this April! Go out with George to look for truck; amazing characters we meet! Claire and Dana have neat time going to Cortland Library. Write brother T. P. and Mary Hauiesen.

Friday, Saturday June 1,2: All these people arrive from New Jersey — Earth People or some such — Plainfield — who came here via Montague having read Steve Diamond's book *What the Trees Said*. Had met Bob and _____ before at Montague — two black guys. A lift to have them around really, tho' they're a little phony, talking about revolution (failed); they want instant solution, etc., but still — like lose 25¢ bet with George as to whether they can fix the chains on the Ford and the gears on the John Deere. They bring along awful food — cookies, etc. Anyway.

Have an amazing day with Claire, as we succeed in really working hard all day and accomplishing exactly nothing! Day started misty and foggy, so no one really got moving until 9. Made blueberry muffins for breakfast. Went out and fooled at length with the John Deere's gears, myself standing around. Got Datson stuck going to get George. Then we preceded to hitch up the manure spreader to a tractor we had lent to us by Popeye's son (Ed Zeuw) with Ira's help. *[Popeye or Zoey was a local who came by often and helped us a lot].* Then, having gotten out there, first chugging up the hill and filling the manure spreader with chicken shit with the Ford, maybe 15 buckets — only to promptly stall the tractor trying to move the shaft that makes the chains flail. Returned with the power wagon and cables to try and restart it — no luck.

By this time its around 1:30 or 2 and we've a snack — Dianne's rye bread and peanut butter. Then we find George who brings out the Datson (more powerful battery) and attaches it by cables directly to the starter to get the tractor started, but we still can't budge the shaft. So shift tractors with Bob (from N.J.) who is spreading phosphate (we had earlier shown him how) and now the long process of attaching the manure spreader to the John Deere. Trouble is you must have the shaft and the hitch the same length. Both are adjustable, but it takes a while to notice that the hitch is (adjustable). The shaft is really hard to do, and I get into kneeling and wacking it with all my might with a rock, for all like a cave man! All this is interspersed with getting various tools, and asking George and Ira questions, long walks to the shop. And then it is intricate to put in the bolt. Finally we attach it, but after no more than a few yards (we do get the shaft to turn around) the bolt that attaches the shaft comes out, and we have to get another. Then Claire stalls the Deere. It takes us a while to get it started, turning this great wheel to do it, Claire actually doing it, beating her chest for George, who by this time is down disking a field with the Zoey tractor (which is also having mechanical troubles). But we don't get too far before we get stuck! The field is too wet! Well, we figure we have to shorten the hitch (we had lengthened it to correspond with the shaft). The increased length of the hitch made it drag in the earth. Then we had to get the Ford to try to move the manure spreader, by this time stuck in deep ruts. One part of the intricacy is you have to lift the manure spreader with the front end loader of the Ford just so the hitch and shafts will connect. Further, by shortening the hitch, the Ford itself got in the way so one had to buttress the manure spreader with rocks. At one point we had to collect some big rocks with the front end loader from the side of the field as smaller ones didn't work.

We finally do it! We go down to the next field (still looks pretty wet) and go along the grass strip, but if you would believe, hardly get to the end before the Deere starts to sputter and lose its power (meaning one of the sparks is plugged)! So we consult George — he tries to fix it without turning off the Deere — spark plug comes slamming out with a bang! We look for it, but cannot find it in the woods along the edge of the field! So that was about it!

Some friends of Claire's came at that point from Massachusetts — opportune — helped a little to prepare supper, but we got diverted by enormous thunderheads and beautiful sky! Bob of Earth comes in after long afternoon of spreading phosphate only to be sent back by George to do last 100 feet. Nice people really, but its hard to see how we can accommodate them, as in fact they number about 24 or 5! Some of the others plant 9 or 10 rows in the kitchen garden. Downpour and much thunder and lightening!

Sunday, June 5: Slept in the barn. Downpour about 7 a.m., like tropics! Make pancakes out of New Hope Mills pancake mix; complain about it (awful bland), but Claire fixes it up by adding molasses, soy flour and blackberries from the freezer. Can't do anything in the fields because of all the wetness. Go with George and Dianne to flea market at Homer. Not too many people there; get an air compressor and some hoes and other stuff from a man with much junk on his truck (and a goat). Stop at Zooey's to pick up tent for Jill. He's there with some local louts drinking beer; tells us of his racing days, and driving some huge machine to make Route 81. Trailer — shows off his dirty stuff, like St. Peter dressed up as a prick. He's always saying God damn this and that, and leering, no not really, but kidding Dianne saying he wants her as a down payment on the tent. Later on at our place when George gently chides Popeye suggesting he not have any more beer, he says "why not!" I've got nothing to live for, etc. etc.

Monday, June 6th: AM BACK IN CAMBRIDGE — UGH — getting somewhat adjusted by the afternoon. Planted with Michael and Rattaree (woman from New Orleans) melons, tomatoes, peppers, morning glories and some other flowers in the front yard. Hope they grow! Am collecting rent. Place looks nice with the screens in, but we never should have undertaken such a quixotic project — they're all handmade by Robert and Jed. I'm told we could have put in adjustable ready-made ones. As it is either the windows are oddly shaped or R. & J. fucked up, as they're gaps in many of the fits. . .

Thursday night June 16: Finally got back here after 10 days in Cambridge. On way there through Wendell people seemed down and ready to come to Willet, but on the way back everyone both at Wendell and Montague up and involved in haying, celery patch, etc., so no recruits. Things much the same here — everything either stuck or breaking down. Somewhat down myself wondering if I shouldn't stick to words and paper and things like a Victorian house in the suburbs with garden, and like tennis anyone!? A portion of a letter to a good friend in Cambridge, noted "not sent" and "goes on to say how nice it is," says the same: Lee: Am sitting out on this farm wondering if after all I shouldn't be content with doing the things I've been brought up to do: tennis, sitting in an office, living in a civilized place, wearing nice clothes, then mountain climbing and canoeing. Later I write in caps: "one might add being married, having kids, etc."

Got here around 2 p.m. — took a walk to see how things looked — new flowers out, etc. Blackberries and raspberries all in bloom. Lots of Indian paintbrush, buttercup still most common, a nice small white flower, some blue ones, all the flowers in the woods gone, as the floor of the forest now entirely shaded.

Loaded chicken manure for Richard, guy from McKee's equipment place who comes after work to spread manure for us with his tractor. Everyone works late — then after supper long session with group from New Jersey who want to camp out in our pine woods in return for labor. Buddhists as Ira calls them — om'd and ah'd over picking stones in Jerry's garden. Long discussion — Ira for, girls against. I'm for them too, as dislike how close we are to not making it for lack of people. Ira and Jill really on me for staying so long in Cambridge — the two N. J. guys didn't stay after all. Am more-or-less persuaded by Dana fifteen would be too many in our pine grove — too bad we can't find a few to integrate into our group. Now we are George, Ira, Jill, Claire, Hamish, Dianne, Dana and me 8 — 9 if you count Richard's nightly visits — he's being paid — not really — only payment he wants it turns out is to maybe use our dump truck — he's slight, gentle, shy, has a cross eye. . .

Friday, June 17: Helped with phosphate, plowed and harrowed today. Actually fixed John Deere with a twig. The line from one spark plug to the distributor broke; couldn't get inside connection, so pushed twig in hole so as to keep it secure—tight. . .

Its raining again — amazing grey black swirling clouds — wind and rain come whipping in just before sunset after long buildup.

This is Saturday morning writing this — Am constipated having not gone to the bathroom since Tuesday. Yesterday worked on the great medieval potato machine! [Designed to cut the seed potatoes into their "eyes"]. Too wet to work in the fields. The machine clacks around — a belt brings the potatoes by the operators who put them into a three department container with place for large potatoes on the sides and one small in the middle which takes the potatoes upwards through knives to cut them into pieces whence they fall onto another belt and into the bags. There are the jobs of loading and unloading, plus watching, as sometimes the knives don't cut the potatoes through. Everyone sort of turned on by this affair, Claire telling us that factory women used to induce orgasms by standing against the moving vibrating belts, so that occasionally above the clacking of the machinery one would be able to hear the oohhss & aahhss!!

Lyn and Andy have arrived, friends of Claire's on their way to Ann Arbor — they work all day with us. Ira, who has gone to New York, brings back with him couple from Argentina. Girl from New York, Betsy, also comes (friend of Claire's), and Pete from

McKee's and a young farmer come for supper. Take people on tour — wild strawberries! Am thick with Lyn breaking one of the unwritten rules around here. She and Andy leave for Ann Arbor Saturday morning.

Saturday, June 16: More work on the potato machine, then helped dig some wet phosphate out of the dump truck, and then got involved doing up the garbage with the front end loader, this being the usual day to go to the dump. Not much doing — again too wet. George and company fail to get our (ex)fire truck to pass inspection, but they go anyway to pick up the potato planter in it. I cook supper, being my turn — brown rice and tuna, beet greens sautéed (small portions of both), corn from the freezer, and hominy grits for dessert with maple syrup — all really good save tuna not so great. Take Dana up to see the sunset, which is nice.

Sunday, June 19: This is kind of a depressing day — really muggy and hot in the morning, still too wet. People get tractors stuck. I can't really get into anything — help Claire and Jane with wet phosphate, then mulch kitchen garden half-an-hour with Dana and her mother (her parents are here), plant also a row of beans (to replace row in which only 3 plants come up — really blank out there). Weed a little with Jane, get some hay for mulching out of the barn with Jill and Dianne. We've been sitting around the table indulging ourselves with ice cream and cake, bread and peanut butter. A couple with a child are visiting, who have an organic farm in the lake region. Talk of various varieties of herbs, and combination plantings to keep various insects away.

　　Crazy night — George does a whole number turning the light off and on like a strobe and shaking to the music — we have a tape courtesy of Hamish. Everyone smokes hashish. Ira reads some poetry in Spanish. Hamish practices out in the barn with the acetylene torch and makes an odd object. Talk with Dana for a while on the loft.

Monday, June 20: Another soggy day — God! Sit around doing not much in the morning. Spend most of the day in the kitchen garden, mulching, etc. Replant various rows where the N. J. people had planted seeds every three feet, apparently mis-understanding the directions regards distance between the rows.

　　Nice in the afternoon — mulched — confronted snake in the garden, I guess not a Copperhead. Tried disking one field late in the afternoon, but promptly sank.

　　Hamish made really good dinner — brown rice, adzuki beans, soybeans, a wild salad—wild mustard greens. He related Claire and I were quite funny out in the kitchen garden putting rotenone on the cabbage, on our knees with butts up in the air trying to identify the plants from the weeds (they're tiny, some having been mostly eaten by flea beetles), saying to one another, "Ah, there's one," etc. . .

In the cathedral that is the barn, things have become romantic with Dana. Don't know where it will go, but for sure the day in the fields cured it!

Tuesday, June 21: Too many things happened today. Phosphate maze — Dana and I shoveled and hoed and stuck screwdrivers in the spreader holes (Dana riding the spreader) all in the way of spreading some rained on phosphate — first rescuing spreader from where it had been stuck. Really took a long time to do not very much, all climaxed when Claire came out to help us finish the long field. Driving along with both Claire and Dana riding the spreader, first the spreader fell off, leaving them behind, then one of the spreader wheels ran over Corn Dog, who was having kind of a fit of vagueness (watched it all happen in slow motion — couldn't do anything) — but Corn Dog not so badly hurt — like mostly OK now — but Dana and I had to carry her off the field to receive much sympathy. Then George got stuck in the Power Wagon. We unhitched and Claire drove over to pull George out. Then this amazing thing happened — while hitching up again the tractor lurched backwards against me, Claire saying she'd done nothing (didn't believe her). Still trying to hitch up I said for her to inch forward. When she did, she couldn't stop the tractor for the clutch on the Deere had broken somehow so that it was permanently engaged! So Claire yelled at me, "Oakes I can't stop it!" as though it were a run-a-way horse. I ran after it to help, fortunately the tractor being good and slow, and turned the choke up so that it stalled. Wow! We could have been really injured if it had gotten stuck in reverse!

Didn't do much else today. Ira's friends from Argentina leave — Hugo and Annamarie. Ira drove all the way to Monticello last night with Claire and Jill. I felt he should have told them, as he went to get his SAAB for them (Hugo and Annamarie) to drive and sight-see before going to Europe. Like being too generous to one's friends. But then I guess Claire and Jill were into going, and Hugo and Annamarie probably liked staying around.

Lets see, did one round with the power wagon pulling the disks. Went to get Richard and unsuccessfully tried to get some chicken shit with the Ford front end loader — too wet — Richard had to go home to get his back hoe!

Its another windy night — romantic — looking forward to homemade granola for breakfast. Stove is out — no gas. Have been working for Ira on Ford with Jill — gas line broke — went down to Clem's so that he might flair the copper line again.

We did really accomplish something today, though I wasn't in on it: the planting of a field of onion sets, radishes and cucumbers, broccoli, marigolds, squash (zucchini), all this companion planting supposedly defeating the bugs!

Everyone has left for various shelters — Claire in the grove, George who has built a neat shack on top of the hill, Jill and Dianne to tent on top of near hill. New girl

(Kathy) from Mass. arrived today, (to bring her horse) with an old dog who almost decapitates Punko, Dianne's tailless neurotic cat, who usually has his confrontations with Foot (another cat) and loud ones too, like a baby's cry!

PHOTO ALBUM
by Claire Alquist

The crowd: Jill, Hugo and Ann Marie, Lynn, Ira, myself.

Ira and Jill and Jill and Ira weeding and/or thinning

IRA! A few joints were smoked!

Oakes — pulling weeds; Dana, Corndog & Hamish

Tail of Hurricane!

<u>Wednesday, June 22</u>: Summer Solstice. RAIN! Sat around most of the day. Took long walk — saw a deer — really large, white flag of a tail. Went into a deserted farmhouse which was empty save for a collection of porno magazines and dairy magazines. Picked wild strawberries, only a few ripe enough.

George and Jill in crazy mood, George wearing his pants so low you could see the top of the triangle of his pubic hair. Jill protests. They all talk of long trip to distant beach and the sun! Actually call the Virginia weather bureau. But they settle for a trip to Mass. *[setting forth in my SAAB]*. Claire pissed off at Jill, as is also Ira, for imposing her will on me to borrow my car (Dianne having a VW which apparently is OK save for slowness).

Long talk in Ira's room about people, especially Jill and Dianne; complaint that they are secretive, and Dianne Jill's slave as it were. Ira wants to reform people, Claire content to let people be. Burlap is trying to get my attention.

Sleep with Dana nude, but we stay from getting into it. Wind and rain — tail of hurricane!

<u>Thursday June 22</u>: Like rain! Work a little on the plumbing and Ford tractor. As to the latter, first we fuck up gas line thing, thinking line flair is stuck there, but instead it is not, and then would you believe lost rubber ring so it still leaks, and we have to go back to Ford place!

Kathy is fun to have around as is affectionate. She's bringing her horse up. We extract Claire's car first in morning — they go to get refrigerator at thrift shop for $25.

Long talk about money. Claire doesn't go for irrational allowance scheme — like Jill takes money from till whenever. Originally we were going to wait until harvest, but Ira agrees principle is that no one should have to spend money while here, and it is legit to get trip money. Claire gets $50 to repay her for various expenses (two months) — (miscarriage cost her $400!). Called up about check coming which was a good thing as Che only sent $57 check (not $2,000 one). *[Connection with Cambridge building]*

Ira and I go to Jerry's — played a little pool and drank beer and peanuts. Jerry talked of exploits. Back at farm people jolly — Hamish stoned/smashed. Still raining out. Great wind at night — edge of hurricane — barn creaked and shuddered! Dana and I huddle together.

<u>Friday, June 23</u>: RAIN. Sleeping in the barn with Dana until late — I'm not sure it makes sense for us to be sleeping together, but so it is. Lets see — to summarize — ate French fries in Cincinnatus (good ones). Got rubber ring mentioned yesterday at McCee's, thus finally fixed tractor, putting cowling back on. Sat around mostly — various people come — Jerry and Alexa to do some welding, actually torching bee hives to clean them. Andy and Lyn back from Ann Arbor, Lyn not getting along so well with her friends there. Long conversation at dinner over Ira's potato pancakes, Claire leading things — referring to contrariness of everyone — tendency to criticize on minute things, etc. Ira gets himself in deep by saying that the way he gets along with people is according to their relationship with their work (to make friends rather) which of course left with him with no woman friends as it were, which is untrue anyway. Like Claire in Amherst whom he calls 'my friend Claire', at whose house now are Hugo and Anna Marie, also George, Jill and Dianne — she *[Claire]* gave Ira and me as well backrubs on one of our trips through. I like her as she says things, like, straight and uses words like *shit* and *fuck* unlike my North Easton friends. Ira also says only reason for commune is economics, community is imported thing. I kid him by saying that's his Marxist bias.

Foote is sitting in my lap purring and putting her paws out on this journal. Clem comes by and tells us all about the floods — the river big and overflowing here, but places in Elmira are 20 feet under water! Hurricane has backtracked into Pennsylvania second time. We're due for two more days of rain — already six inches!

<u>Saturday, June 24</u>: Not so much rain today, but cloudy and cold most of the day — rain off and on though not heavy. Lyn and Andy leave — wrong, Lyn and Claire leave for a few days. We — Dana, Cathy, Ira and I go to Dawes Hill. They have yurts, work horses, a meditation TeePee, everything built in a circular or octagonal style. People seem with it — nice garden, they've goats and chickens — more like Wendell and Montague. We stop for pizza. Dana and I finally talk to each other last night which makes it better for us. We had kind of agreed that I make up my own place and split, but the very talking about it made things better so I haven't moved yet. It wasn't just me that wouldn't touch her in the day — it turns out also to be her — the group pressure against one to one relationships. Having talked we are more relaxed. Still — anyway trip is fun. We (really Dana, Ira and I) agree its nice not to have George, Jill and Dianne around. They, especially Jill, kind of thwart conversation — expression of feeling, etc.

We get back to find Jill, Dianne and George back. They ran into a deer so as to damage my car badly enough so as to have to tow it back! My insurance is $250 deductible (3 or $400 damage to the radiator, etc.). Fortunately nobody hurt — the deer dead — Jerry skins it. They have a good trip otherwise. Dace, Betsy & Steve

Diamond may come out. Have a long talk with George who explains some of Jill's uptightness, and his own as well. Revolves around their having to spend the long winter there, and Jill being afraid people will phase her out of what she has struggled for as it were. George tells her best thing is to welcome people, and show your position by showing interest in the farm (as Ira does, Dana and I suggest). Talk to George smoking dope until virtually dawn! He has this idea of people getting together. . .

Sunday, June 25: Dana and I don't get up until noon. Help Kathy unload shit from barn in the process showing her how to drive the tractor. Sit around, munching on good granola Kathy makes, and Dianne's Indian pudding. We have group discussion about money, Jill calling it, as distressed to learn from George people resentful of her privileged status. Forgot to record Ira, Dana and I had earlier discussion with Claire in which Ira said he'd assumed it was understood everyone got living expenses, which would include trips to places, etc. Ira makes out check to Claire for $50 (expenses since April) which satisfies her. Anyway, as with Claire conversation, there was talk of setting an allowance at a certain amount per week or month so that people wouldn't have to justify, say, smoking cigarettes. But everyone seems to come around to Ira's view that best to let it come up as needed, and that it shouldn't needn't be looked on as like asking parents for money. We don't have enough to swing allowance idea. Speaking of money, received $2,600 from sale of Ocean Science *[a stock]* — paid back Gerry and Kaysie's loan. Was going to go through all the bills and check books to find out what we're spending on what, but only got a little way into it. $174 telephone bill arrives.

Note: I did find a typed Agreement of Partnership folded in the Journal which had everyone contributing $100 at the beginning of the season to buy seeds and supplies, and which did spell out that people should live for free for the summer, to be paid a dollar a day for expenses. The $100 was to be returned at the end of the season, and any surplus divided equally amongst the people who worked at the farm. You were expected if not "required" to take a day off entirely away from the farm and work once a week. The first sentence read, "I hereby undertake to work with us this summer planting, weeding, harvesting, plowing, doing construction, cooking and whatever else at the farm . . . mostly for the joy of it and to do it."

The agreement also contained some language about assuming the risk of injury. I myself had drafted it (law background) and people generally agreed to it, but then no one paid any attention to it whatever thereafter. Back to Sunday, June 25:

Sun comes out! Dana and I go for walk. Flowers beautiful — daisies, buttercups — we listen to bobolinks, and watch them burble their song in the sun. We listen to a catbird and thrasher sing, a field sparrow, get real close look at a yellowthroat. But then its best when we go over to the woods which Dana hadn't seen — has magical aspect — wood thrush sounds as though its in an echo chamber, very beautiful as well, also hear the downward spiral of the veery, and see a redstart.

Back — Kathy freaked out, giving Ira the business (disadvantaged by having his pants down), saying things like all you do is work, and ignore emotions completely — lose ourselves in work just like parents! Much laughter, but she's serious to an extent.

Monday, June 26: Not raining at last, but still cloudy, but by now, evening, it is clear, and there is a full moon — orange! We actually worked today! Carried or rather pulled all the sacks of potatoes *[the cut up eyes]* up to the barn floor to dry out as they're starting to rot with the wet weather (some 100 bags).

Drove, towing SAAB to garage. Estimate $350 — hood, grill, one light, radiator, fan belt damaged.

Really nice in the fields — pick wild flowers and strawberries.

Tuesday, June 27: Fountain pen yet! George just cooked a dinner of milkweed (good), horse radish greens, potato soup, peanut butter cookies, and nettle tea (not so good). Pretty idle day — in fact did very little. Helped George put the cultivators on the H — he got stuck with them in the corn field. Helped Ira a little with the black plastic mulch layer, unloaded with Ira phosphate from the red truck, shoveled a few wood shavings with Kathy and Dana for K's horse which seems to be really arriving in a day.

Went for walk by myself down through the woods to the river — really nice having the sun out! Went swimming in the river — cold and much current.

Thought about where I am — can't think I can write it down — revolves around fact I'm 39 so maybe I should make it with people my age and experience, for all how neat Ira and George are. Thought about (abstract doodle). MADE LOVE WITH DANA.

Wednesday June 28: Beautiful day! Begins at an early hour as got awakened at about 4 by Kathy's horse arriving, which proved at 8:30 when we got up to be a very handsome horse — red/brown, friendly, big. Kathy road off on him bareback, jangling to his trot. Then just a moment later we saw two deer out the kitchen window.

Am sitting writing this on a bench in front of the house with Dana, who is also writing hers, half watching the usual show out front which is Corn Dog and a sweet tiny puppy whom we call Puppetro and various variations. I see I have neglected to write about him — her rather — what a dog! She's so clumsy falling down all the time like on the slippery bank of a stream, and her typical pose is belly up. Sometimes she'll hold a bone in her paws like hands. Puperdo she's just called by Dianne. Mandarin is the name Hamish says — he's indefatigable — playing with c.d. *[another dog]*.

Actually worked today — weed detail out in the corn fields — once over lightly on field George had cultivated, occasionally unearthing corn plants covered over by mis-cultivation resulting from wetness in the field. Then, after a Hamish salad, returned to the field which is badly grown over with morning glory vines—bindweed. Endless job. George says we could use a few niggers. Language is not too cool around here. We joked about my lying down position *[weeding]* — what would the foreman say.

Went skinny-dipping in the river, me and Jill and Dianne, Dana and Kathy. Went upstream and surprised them floating by in the current. Kathy says being out here is like childhood relived, which of course it is! Claire and Lyn come back late — much talk.

Thursday, June 29: Weeding was the order of the day — three rows each George says — pulling the bindweed out of the corn. Around one or two starts to spit rain. Got to feeling dizzy somehow, so took long nap. Tractors starting up again — harrowing, cultivating — maybe starting planting tomorrow.

Friday, June 30: RAIN AGAIN! — FUCK — Stayed in bed with Dana really late. Sat around a long time. Finally went on a walk. Talked with Dan and Michelle. George and crowd go to Pennsylvania. Girls go to Ithaca. Think maybe I'll go back *[to Cambridge]* tomorrow. Doesn't look too good for us. We still haven't planted our potatoes, nor any of our greenhouse plants (peppers, tomatoes and melons) and the corn isn't very high — 3 or 4 inches — too much water too little sun. The small vegetables we planted (beets, carrots, turnips, radishes) probably are washed away. — The seed bed is probably OK (broccoli, lettuce, cauliflower, some of which doesn't have to be transplanted). For all that we'll probably still make it, but now we'll have to wait a few days before getting out in the fields.

Saturday July 1: Weeded all day pulling bindweed out of the cornfield. Sun comes out! Everybody visited, it being Saturday, like Richard and Pete. George tried to talk them into weeding, but of course they'd have none of it. Curt, the dapper man George knows from the flea markets — wanted to know who was sleeping with whom. Hamish had a visitor (female) who bought us some yummy ice-cream, and Hugo and Ann-Marie, Ira's friends from Argentina came, on the back of a red truck saying they'd sold Ira's car for money — it didn't make the hill because of a bad clutch. They made us supper of rice and potatoes and chicken (good — first meat yet here — a la Argentina). Then we had a business meeting, which was quite gloomy in a way, to the point that we will need to make about 10 thousand to break even! Last year we made $1,500 gross! But come good weather!

Forgot to mention another visitor, Herb, friend of Dianne's, whom I took on the grand tour eating strawberries as we went out.

After supper some dope was smoked and beer drunk — and we had a show as it were outside — like George sang some ancient 40s crooners song (like Star Trek), and did a Charleston, and Ira and I did a strange show, Ira imitating a monkey and then knighting me with a dead plant, and Burlap took part grabbing the sword from my hand as I rushed after Ira, who by that time was imitating a I don't know what, and I was into doing a strange thing with my foot, dragging it on the ground digging my big toe in the dirt. The finale of the show was Ira driving the tractor (Ford) around and around in front of us — lights on etc., with the harrows still attached — quite a spectacle! The above reminds me that one of Ira's sayings is "what y a call it" which me (and others too) have been into saying too.

The stars were out which was amazing — we looked at Scorpio — you could see the entire Milky Way. Then the moon came up, a half moon, but bright, and we all walked up the hill to look at it.

Sunday, July 2: A sunny day! We all get up early. I made the rounds to get everybody up which took about half an hour plus, George being way on top of the hill, Kathy in the pine grove, etc. Dana made some pancakes. In spite of an early start (7 a.m.) not too much got done very soon (lazy Sunday). Hoed out in the seed bed amongst the lettuce and broccoli, and later hoed up in the kitchen garden, and later still — after a really nice swim in the river, all of us letting ourselves be taken by the current, and basking in the sun along the banks (climbed a tree naked), Hamish, Herb, Dianne, Dana and George going swimming — weeded in another corn field, more grass than bind weed, finding two beautiful small satin white moths.

Hamish cooked a fine dinner of vegetable curry, lentils, onions and everything in it. We sat out after to view the sunset (mackerel sky) and confer about the fact no one washes the dishes of breakfast and lunch, and to plan tomorrow when we are to plant all our melons, tomatoes and peppers.

Ira and I have a big fight again after I push watermelon in his face for saying "nigger" — real wrestling! Ira and George are out in the barn (10 p.m. approx) making a stabilizing bar for the 3-point hitch on the Ford, which somehow had gotten lost.

Monday, July 3: Mackerel sky night before turns out not to be sailor's delight as it is raining at 6:30 when we are all supposed to be up. Ira is pissed anyway at all of us for not getting up — the rain is a drizzle, and so we plant the melons, laying the plastic mulch, loading the hay wagon with the flats. I get to keep records as transplanted (rather planted) a good part of them way back in the spring. The black plastic (heat is the main thing, but also the melons lay on it, and of course no weeds) is layed by a device which tucks it under earth on both sides — about 4 feet wide — then someone makes a hole with a pipe, and someone else puts a plant by each hole (they're in pea pods), and then they get planted — Burpee, Harper, Main Rock, Kasakah, Penn Sweet, Classic, etc.

Rain finally gets to us in the afternoon — we go in to eat French fries. We go back out for a late session, and back for potato pancakes by Ira.

Kathy talks to me — why don't I talk to Ira? In one way or another we are not equals — like he's been on these farms so long — (like my mentor). Ira has been kind of uptight, partly because Kathy has kicked him out of her bed, feeling that he's too heavy sexually. Stereo gets played which changes the mood. Looks like rain tomorrow — I'll be going back to Cambridge.

July 4th, Cambridge & North Easton, Hitch Hiking

July 4th, Tuesday, might have been a really nice day, for it stopped raining and it was as Dana says a Peter Max sky, elaborate clouds, cool, really like fall. But Richard came by with some firecrackers, and talked Ira into throwing a firecracker into the kitchen, which really made me see red, so I walked out there with my coffee cup in hand saying "you fucker" (of course imagining Ira to be the sole instigator) and threw the hot coffee into his face! Wow! That was really sumpin! We fought for a little while and then stopped. I guess violence breeds violence, and there is a certain part of Ira that is uncontrolled violence which I reacted to. It was sort of tragic, tho', for it was circumstantial — Richard had talked him into it — he sure split in a hurry! He was on his back end loader and out of there before you could say 'what-a-ya-call-it'. Actually Ira was in a good mood — Kathy had talked to him the night before and they had gotten things together.

Well, the day didn't seem so nice after that — did up a few melons / helped Claire set up with watermelons, keeping records and all. Got a ride with Herb (Dianne's friend) around 3:30. On the road, helped drive, going through the Catskills. He left me off near New Haven on the Merritt Parkway. Got a ride almost immediately — weird being on that road again. Ride left me off in Hartford — walked across the bridge, and after not too long got a ride with a Harvard student into Cambridge. [Written July 10th — reference 'weird' refers to the many times I had been on the Merritt Parkway under different circumstances!]

July 5 - 7: Went out to North Easton with Mother. Had amazing [luxurious] meal of steak, fresh peas and summer squash at David Ameses — spent the night there.

Showed Mother around Brookline Street — some flowers are up, pretty haphazard — tomatoes up, peppers and squash doing badly — some 'grass' plants out there. Talked to various people in the building. Craig *[Ace]* suggested maybe I ought to tend to the building instead of playing farmer — he was a little pissed at being taken for granted in respect to taking care of the building — think we cleared that up. Went by the office *(Conservation Law Foundation)* to read all my mail. Had lunch on the Common with Gerry and Kaysie *[Ives, my ex-neighbors from the South End]*. Visited the Law Commune — got kind of offered a job as an investigator would you believe!

June 8th: Decided not to stay too long, so set forth Saturday to hitch to Wendell and hence to Willet. Forgot to say had dinner with Jarlath and Joannie, and Jarlath may come out to the farm, Joannie going to Spain. Took me about five rides to get out to Wendell, and walked in from Miller's Falls (2 or 3 miles). Usual crowd there — had dinner — spent long time talking to this 19 year old friend of Marguerite's brother Kenny — amazing tales of dope and sex — they had been selling the Green Mountain Post *[newsletter/magazine put out by Wendell and Montague Farms]* in Harvard Square to raise money for the mortgage.

Kenny decides to come out with me, so next morning we set forth. CE gives us a ride to Route 2 at Turner's Falls on his way to a Reeves race *[reference?]*. After sitting there for some time with no takers, this cop comes up and does a little number with us, asking all sorts of questions, me sitting there quaking a little as I have some dope in my jacket pockets! The funny thing was he stopped someone else, and we got a ride from that person. We heard bad things about the cop from him and the next person he picked up, a real pig they said.

Anyway, took us about five rides to get out to Williamstown. There we waited a long time, and walked a ways before getting a long ride down Route 20. Stopped by a farmhouse on Route 26 and bought a ½ peck of peas, shelling half of them for a snack waiting for another ride. Got a ride into Cortland where a whole bunch of kids having a party helped us get a ride. Got to Willet after various other adventures — this guy stopped off at a kind of junk yard to get a part, and later in his violence swerved to run over a rabbit — arrive around 8:30, some 10 or 11 hours! Back with Dana — long talk!

Monday, July 10: RAIN. Got up late and didn't do much. Went for a walk picking wild strawberries — not too good because of the rain — bland. Sun sort of comes out. Work for a while in the kitchen garden — plant a row of onion sets. All the tomatoes and peppers are planted, did I say? Tomatoes look awful, but George says they'll live. Lets see — Dana's brother David here. Lyn is having hassle with Ira and people over work, and fact Ira's boss, etc., Kathy in the middle. This all gets talked about as we go out to Marathon to have some coffee.

Tuesday, July 11: POTATOES! Ira gets us up early, like 7 a.m. Unload potatoes and transfer these big bags of potatoes and phosphate around, from one truck to another and onto the potato planter, which gets pulled along by the chugging John Deere, and has a seat for someone to sit and stir the potatoes and phosphate with a so-called potato stick. A potato magnate *[farmer]* came the day before to show us how — amazed to find an all girl crew. We all sit around and talk awaiting something or other. Kathy draws this amazing analogy between our microcosm and society in general in respect to sacrifice each individual has to undergo — the coopting of revolutionaries, etc., all in relationship to Lyn's rocking the boat. Ira wants to kick her out — wants not all this feminist talk, like farming is the thing. As Kathy is interested in learning farming, she is somewhat on Ira's side (of course as well as sleeping with him). George sick today — Ira, George and Lyn (guess tension must have eased) talking about writing an article for Rodale in order to buy a large tractor.

More potatoes in the afternoon; didn't work so hard as the machine breaks down a couple of times. Sat around, once copying Burlap by lying down under the truck watching the flowers and the grass and the sky. Orange fritillary butterflies are quite abundant. Later we went on a wild mushroom hunt with Kenny, Kathy and the dogs. Poor Dana, both Corn Dog and her tiger cat are in heat, the cat making amazing noises. Kenny gives us the lowdown on the mushrooms — he goes by taste — peppery taste means poisonous, also the appearance - like the death veil!

Wednesday, July 12: Got up late — *do I please you?* Nice to be up late not doing much after the frenzy of yesterday. Planted some cucumbers with Claire and Kathy. Hot out. Late in the afternoon we all went swimming. Good dinner by Hamish. I cleaned the stove and defrosted the icebox, the stove really gross, to do my part around the kitchen, Claire really disturbed about it. Talk with Kathy and Claire about power structure — Ira and George.

Graven Haynes and his son, ex potato growers (1 mile by 6 mile farm) come by to drink beer, and held by the charm of George and company stay until at least one or two. Even Hamish gets drunk. Find it hard to relate to such locals — nice enough and eager to know us, but straight — too straight! "Do you play acid rock all the time??" . . .

Thursday, July 13: More planting — cucumbers. Hamish planted some zucchini with the planter. Took Corn Dog for a walk. Went with Dana and found a nice patch of wild strawberries. Got pissed at George for he waited so long on the transplanting of the broccoli, ignoring this huge thunderstorm, so that found myself transplanting them in the rain — cursed him! Reminds me of George *[brother]* mercurial — no self-consciousness, eternal optimist and doer. Everyone a little up tight. Hamish takes off for his spot of civilization in Clinton. George, sensing the mood, forgets about the broccoli (though the rain stops) and we all go to Norwich to the movies, along with Jerry and Clem, who happens to drop by. Expect to see *Casablanca,* but instead we get to see *Sahara,* an awful war movie, though with Bogart, which I'd seen a year before on T.V. We all smoke my dope on the way over, and of course everyone becomes thoroughly stoned! Weirdly the audience is all from some teenage camp (who laughed in all the wrong places), no locals there. We return to have a little pumpkin pie which I'd made out of frozen filling from last year.

Friday, July 14: Planted some of the broccoli early which had been left out in the rain, but which proved to be in vain, as news is that they have club root, which will be fatal to all of them!! So whole crop is kaput! George speaks to various farmers trying to get seedlings, but no luck. We had hoped to plant an acre and gross about $2,000 off them.

So — we go out and plant onion sets in rows, and plant the rest of the field in small veggies, doing some of the dirt covering by hand as the planter doesn't quite make it.

Drive into Cortland with Kathy to get my car fixed at last — they needed the money so I had to get the check certified. Talk at length about George and Willet. . .

Come back to help further with planting, eating at dark. Jerry is by as well as a friend of George's, his wife and boy — his family's mailman. His son, maybe 8, hugs him occasionally, and they tell tales of the flooding.

Ira and Jill come back late having spent a couple of days out visiting Ira's Aunt Rose in Monticello, and then going down to New York — the beaches, etc., partly to cure Ira's hay fever. Ira's Aunt Rose sends up a bunch of goodies — tuna fish, sardines, etc., they have done nothing but eat in the two days, they relate. Ira also brings up some clams he'd dug! Jill talks to me briefly, serious, asks me if I ever wanted to be an excellent lawyer, etc. She talks about her background and how competitive it is, middle class values, etc. Per usual she pretty much controls things, deciding when to begin and close conversation, and I am a little uneasy with her. — They have brought along an English girl Wendy, who may stay with us for a while, and Dianne's friend Herby also arrives for the weekend with crates of oranges and plums.

We have in FACT for all practical purposes _finished_ planting! There's no more prepared land to plant. Now we'll need to cultivate and weed soon as some of the corn really needs it.

<u>Saturday, July 15</u>: Got up around 8:30 to wash the dishes which had told Dana would do, and to take a shit which forgot to yesterday. Sit around most of the morning feeling a little shitty. Received check from insurance company turning out to be only $50 less than the damage — had had to send it to the State Street Bank for their endorsement. Worked in the kitchen garden this afternoon shoveling up a row for peas and hoeing.

Amazing happenings in the evening. Clem comes over at nightfall, and asks Kenny of Jill's whereabouts, which Kenny unwisely tells him (up in her tent on the hill). About 20 minutes later Clem and Jill come back, and Clem departs to drive up to George's tent. Jill is all shaken up, and is angry with Kenny, for Clem has tried to put the make on her, and forcefully at that. Not rape, like, but enough to make Jill scared and disgusted. She was sitting in front of the tent waiting, among other things with her blouse open. After that tale, which was shocking, Jill goes on to talk about other local types — Popeye for example — and Claire suddenly sees that Popeye's fatherly attitude towards her —"Don't let those guys make a slave of you," really means — 'you're already puttin' out for those guys fucking them, so you shouldn't have to work for them as well' — Claire also tells tales of the potato growers who had come by the other night where after she had been friendly, she said good night, and went off towards the barn, she heard the guy behind here saying, "Claire," obviously expecting some action, so she came back to the kitchen — how woman's lib got started!

Bill Lattimore, another local, was there for all of this (college graduate he differentiated himself as) — told about Popeye, after meeting him up here once, how he told him afterwards what an awful place this was, how fucked up, etc.

Then we talked about the riff that had developed between Claire and I and others versus George, Ira and Jill — most enlightening. Both Claire and I kind of sided with and attached ourselves to the newcomers when they came, Claire, because, partly, she wanted them (women) to be equal, me I guess simply because I am easy to relate to, and because in a certain way I was rebellious of the authority of Ira, George and Jill. Before all the newcomers came, we had a fairly tight group: Ira, Jill, George, Claire, Hamish and I, but too new and not strong enough to withstand the impact of all the new people. Among other things Dianne came, and Jill attached herself to her. For Claire, she suddenly saw she was ceasing to relate to the farm as a learning experience — hadn't talked to Ira for weeks, etc. Same for me — we got to bed around 3 a.m.

Also talked to Ira today. He sees things quite simply — this place is a farm, not a commune! Some people <u>are</u> more equal than others, namely the permanent residents — Ira, George, Jill and me (?). People should be here to learn farming, not to be a commune; furthermore we're all so disparate, no commune is possible.

Sunday— This is now Tuesday, July 18, and everything seems calmer and less crazy because there are only four of us — Ira, Claire, Jarlath and I. Lets see: Kathy and Kenny go Monday to Amherst (Kenny to Wendell and then to Asheville), Hamish and Wendy go Tuesday morning for Canada to visit Hamish's cousins, and on dropping back here will go on to the West, California, etc., and they take along with them Lyn, who has decided to leave too late to get a ride with Kathy, they to drop her off in Utica (N. Y. Thruway). Then Jill leaves for Philly giving Dana a ride as her folks live near there (Dana finally deciding to have Corn Dog spayed taking her down in the morning). Dog situation tough, Burlap mooning over her and CD all freaked out from being cooped up in a small room. Then George gets it together to drive down to the Keys! Florida Keys! —with Dianne and her VW — they have a friend down there with a schooner, etc., — leaving us after cooking us a real nice dinner of noodles and river clams and milkweed and ice tea with wild mint.

But back to Sunday: Sunday brings all these people (!) like George's parents who come bringing much food and further tales of floods. Clem is around as aforesaid, and the delicatessen man we did the barn roof for last year comes by [farm side business last year]. Then of all things Jarlath, my acquaintance from Cambridge comes! In his ancient Ford. He promptly gets into things — we go down for a skinny dip in the river, but our first trip doesn't make it as we're met by a virtual wall of rain coming down the driveway — it looks for a moment as though we can back up fast enough to avoid it! Then everyone goes folk dancing in Ithaca, including Jarlath at the last moment. I am lonely and wishing I had gone, but took dogs for a walk, and it was nice sitting around with Ira and Kathy and Lyn. Lyn is sick and has been really for a week. Ira cooks up one of his patented omelets, with tuna fish and carrots and many condiments. Talked and watched a little news and Charlie Chan (ugh) on TV. No work done today. George was going to cultivate, but too wet. People have fun at folk dance — ours almost the main group. Don't get to sleep until at least two.

Monday (July 17): Nice sunny day — hot! Work up in melon patch putting stones and earth around the plants on the plastic to keep it down. Kenny gets us all together for a swim — really nice in the sun and at midday instead of too late (yesterday in the clouds we had played tag). Today we're like a nudist camp — 8 or 10 of us!

Finished the plastic and did a little work in the kitchen garden — not much. Help cook dinner with Wendy making a blueberry pie out of partially fermented berries from the freezer (fair), and helping Wendy with her brown rice dish. Wendy is into riding — had wanted to teach riding here (the U.S.), and of all things gets her first chance teaching Jill on Enterprise the next day.

Monday night talk with Lyn — she's leaving. Among other things she gets turned on by Jerry, arch male chauvinist that he is. She's depressed and confused as he'll have nothing to do with her after once coming over to say good night to her. . .

Tuesday (July 18) — already mentioned something about it. Help Lyn with her tent, and watch various people go. Spend some time cultivating the tomatoes and peppers (between the plastic, driving the Ford). Then we all go swimming — then more cultivating — I am very leisurely at it. Some depressed and musing where I might ought to be and how to get out of being here!

Help Dianne a little plant flowers in the front yard, and go to Cincinnatus with Jarlath for ice cream. I feel better now — somehow having fewer people makes it nicer. We have a nice talk, the four of us (Ira, Claire, Jarlath and I) deciding what to do tomorrow and generally about female's plight up in these sticks. Jarlath admits to liking Lyn, as he's insecure, and she's obviously insecure female. Claire admits she just couldn't deal with Lyn's problems — too much work to be done — there are better places for her.

Wednesday, July 19—really hot muggy day. Claire cultivates; Jarlath hoes in the kitchen garden; I get into cleaning up the living room and putting up screens, none of which thought I could do yesterday. Cultivate one row (with the Ford) mowing down about a tenth of the row — not so easy — the weeds are really thick — the set up is difficult as there are two discs turned at an angle with only 4 to 6 inches leeway, also the teeth of the cultivator. We go swimming, and then load up the hay wagon for mulching the kitchen garden. Put up more screens; I make an instant screen door by kicking out the four panels of the kitchen outside door and attaching screen!

Enterprise the horse was a little put out today, for Jarlath fed him sawdust instead of grain, not understanding our directions and being a little spaced out — that was for breakfast — he gets fed three times a day.

Slept in Claire's tent out by the grove — mosquitoey, a little claustophobic — but nice to hear the birds sing in the morning instead of just English sparrows and the barn swallows.

Thursday, July 20—another hot one, though not as bad as yesterday — a little breeze. Sun up when I get up, fog boiling up from the valley. Picked peas, not prolific, but enough for an Ira pea omelet!

Attached up the brush hog to the Ford (like a huge rotary lawn mower), and cut the hay out front, partly for our volleyball court and soccer field, no longer any good for hay as gone to seed, and not so good anyway. Cut the soccer field specially. Nice smell from cutting it. Went through a whole bank of purple thistle-like flowers, which picked some for the kitchen [a bouquet].

Went swimming — Ira, Jarlath and I. Worked some in the kitchen garden, Jarlath talking about some of the people in my Cambridge building. Claire picks up Corn Dog from the vets — big dog scene, Burlap much attached still, Borsche barking away as he tries to hump her. Dana called while Claire was away — tells me she's written me a letter, which I expect will be in the way of a 'Dear John'.

Friday, July 21: Not much doing today. Slept in George's shelter last night — really comfortable. Sat around. Bacon and eggs a la Ira. Jim Aaron came last night [back-to-the-lander from near Wendell]. Likes our house as ancient, and like an Appalachian shack. Took Jarlath on the grand tour. Went for drive to get plumbing parts and to borrow a ladder from Danny to do the upstairs screens, our ladder not being long enough. Our sink I fixed yet! [Dan Mullins is the lone alternative-type person in the town of Willet—he owns a large barn where he keeps a collection of antiques of a kind].

Ira got it up to fix the brakes on the SAAB which are gone. Right in the middle of it the jack slipped and the car fell on Ira's foot! God! Jim who was nearby came running and we lifted the car off his foot. Not so bad — bad bruise though.

Went swimming. Fed the dogs. Broke up Burlap and Corn Dog. Put Enterprise in his stall. Beautiful evening — the heat wave is broken. George Sherman visits [from Wendell]. We're sitting watching a late movie on TV.

Am back in the barn for the night as Jim and Claire are up on the hill. All the dogs are transfixed by Corn Dog, and stay around the house all night, all panting for her favor. Some power! Fights going on, Burlap 'protecting' her, etc.

Saturday, July 22: If yesterday was like Sunday, today was certainly a working day. Though still leisurely — worked on the SAAB. Actually put in the new brakes — not really such a difficult job! Though put a little knick in the disk trying to knock out the dent on the wheel from falling off the jack. Went to Cincinnatus to get horse feed. Weeded and thinned a whole row of carrots in the kitchen garden (about a couple of hours) then drove to Prebble [perhaps 30 miles away, near Cortland] to get these broccoli and cauliflower plants we had ordered. Nice old farmer — got to talking when he discovered we were organic. One would do well under organics, he said, if there were half the population and people worked twice as hard. He also described how people had gotten fussy after the advent of the chain store — not standing for cabbage worm [damage] which once was accepted. Described how the worm originally only affected the plants on the outside of the field. Perhaps nature would have taken care of it if no spray — he was certain of it in fact.

Drove back — we had a Coke on the way — back to summers of old! Went swimming. Then I let Jarlath talk me into a hamburger before finally going out on the field to plant the broccolis and cauliflowers. Little b's, big c's — we planted the former first, and didn't get through them quite — in amongst the small veggies.

Sunset nice — mosquitoes out. . .

Jim [Aaron] cooks up some of last year's kidney beans — really good for a basic bad bean (over-ripe?). Jim Ord was by, also some bee people. We are to house their hives. We all sit around the table and talk of bees and honey. Went to the Beaver for one drink — half hoping to meet Karen whom I'd met in town today — most people drunk — women in shorts yet. Come back for Jim's blueberry pie of which I'd made the crust, the berries picked at Bob Adams, the junk Jehovah's Witness guy.

George Sherman to whom I've been talking tells me to write down that you still can't smoke a joint at the kitchen table (due to the presence of the bee people).

Great thunderstorm — late at night.

Sunday, July 23: Everything changes around here so fast — like today a bad day for me — hated it — couldn't get into doing anything, or not doing anything! Finally helped Ira in a desultory way put teeth on the Ford cultivator. Trouble I figure is that our numbers fell below the threshold number, for Jim left with their friend Julie, who brought him, and Jarlath left for N.J. to say good bye to Joannie (his girl friend who did pay rent to me [Brookline Street] and now is going to Spain) giving George Sherman a ride towards Ithaca. But Kathy comes in the afternoon — after planting a few broccolis, ended that planting. I can't believe more than a few will live — they look awful. We have for lunch a vegetable thing from our garden — sautéed turnips, peas (pea pods some of them), green onions, plus store-bought celery and carrots which Claire did.

We go out again to find clouds in the sky (had been blue skies, fairly warm with wind blowing). Cauliflowers are looking good, much bigger than the broccolis, and we finally get into it (everyone else lazy like me too) until we are interrupted by a heavy cloudburst — all run for cover.

Ira comes and picks up Claire, Cathy and I in the Datsun. Rain stops after a while.

Cathy and I go out to plant some more — truly spectacular sunset. Ira and Claire work on the tractor cultivator — Super C — for the hydraulics had given out. We continue to plant into the moonlight talking about whether or not Willet is an escape from "reality" — as in the outside world — politics. Cathy believes you cannot separate ones life from politics. We cook up some soda biscuits to eat with honey.

<u>Monday, July 24</u>: Amazing day — like October — great clouds all over the place, blue sky, windy, clear, cool. Made some blueberry pancakes for breakfast, after which we set forth to plant the rest of the cauliflower plants. Rest of the day (that took about an hour and some) did virtually nothing*.   Contemplated some things like screening the second floor, and fixing up this rickety ladder — maybe tomorrow. Tried cultivating the melons, but promptly broke Ira's homemade teeth. Went to Cincinnatus to deposit the insurance check that had arrived for the SAAB (signed by the State Street Bank). Talked to Kathy at length — relationships, communities, Ira — went with her to Cincinnatus to get some ice cream. Worked a little in the kitchen garden.

Watched great sunset. Feel somehow ill disposed — too much ice cream? Went with Ira on the tractor to look around — potatoes just coming up, zucchini going strong. Jill called and will stay away a few more days. Dana will probably stay through the weekend as her parents (mother and step father) are having a rough time.

*as did everyone — all flaking out after lunch. . .

<u>Tuesday / Wednesday / Thursday July 25-7</u>: Not much doing. Ira worked on the hydraulics of the Super C which broke, having to take apart the whole tractor practically. I did some screening, and fixed up this rickety ladder — aluminum on rotten wood, but couldn't really stand on it. Spent quite a bit of time putting teeth on the Ford harrow. Ira had been working on them, welding, etc. Broke three on the first run, so Claire got some new ones on a trip to Cortland. Then in the afternoon, with a great thunderstorm in full view across two valleys, finished cultivating the melons between the black plastics.

Nancy and David, locals, came by one night — we went out for ice cream with their VW bus, Claire along. Great night, full moon, huge black cloud, wind. Somehow we got into talking ghosts and spirits, and I mentioned the footsteps Dana and I heard in the barn on the roof. This really freaked out Claire, who it turns out had heard them also. It freaked her out particularly because Kathy had told her at length of a ghost at a stable she had had her horse at. The ghost apparently had power over the horses, so that once when Kathy came late at night into the stables, she felt the horses were definitely hostile to her, as though she were interrupting a séance! This all got to me as well, so that I too decided not to sleep in the barn. When I went there to turn the lights off, I felt plain frightened like I did not since I was 8 or whatever! Claire slept with Ira and Kathy; I went up to George's shelter — nice out in the moon and weather, but really cold.

The next night slept in the barn again, as did Claire, deciding to cool it as it were, but Enterprise made so much noise that Claire came over to my section, sleeping in my blue sleeping bag. Claire and Kathy got to see a calf get born at Clem's, and liked it that his family was affectionate with one another.

Worked on the SAAB the next day with Ira. He made a tool an "extractor" to take off the wheel with the arc welder and acetylene torch — neat — only it turned out the brakes were OK. Claire put a muffler on her Bug. Dana comes back — go to pick her up in Binghamton. Much talk — Kathy re Ira's ideas — he's a bootstrap guy: people should be self-sufficient — don't molly coddle people, etc. Jill just arrives. . .

Friday, July 28: Had a kind of interesting morning talking to some locals (Donna and Roddy) about how they found God, and quit drinking and smoking and wanting to commit suicide! She described power of "love" flowing out of her husband's hands to another man, etc.

Hamish and Wendy arrive and leave (I write a letter for them). George and Dianne come back from Palm — no Key West! Talked to Mark Kramer on the phone. I didn't do anything today! Though contemplated such projects as putting up screening, lubricating the Ford, cultivating (did do about 4 rows before I fucked it up).

I want out again! Fuck!

Later, after writing this, did clamor up my rickety jerry-built ladder to put a few screens in as the sun setting. Today is Saturday — feel better today, though did virtually nothing save walk through the fields with George. He went through Key West with a kind of wrap around cloth — good really for hot weather, but he got some bad looks and vibes here and there. George and Dianne titter and joke.

Finally got into putting away the potato planter, but of course perhaps should have followed the motto "leave well enough alone", for hosing it off filled up one part with water and wet rock phosphate, so had to remove two bins to extract the water, and oiling it with old engine oil might be easy with a spray rig, but not so easy with a paint brush.

Well, go tomorrow — wish in a way I wasn't. . .

August — Sojourn to North Easton & Georgia, Wendell

Monday, August 8: Am back here! Having spent two weeks away — too long! Usual awfulness of adjusting again. Thought about Willet last few days — wanted to communicate but too difficult as I was in other people's houses. Went to Georgia! Beautiful heat — inspired by George and Dianne. Traveled down there with a friend Jean to rescue another friend Lyn. But it turned out when we got there that Lyn was satisfied with her move. Still it was a nice visit — went out to St. Simon's Island with all its estates, most in ruins, moss draped Live Oaks everywhere. Went out to North

Easton to visit the Ericsons, who have a beautiful garden and an Emily Dickenson daughter. Visited Steve and Beth who have a very nice country place in Acton. Of course caught things up in Cambridge.

On the way out to Willet spent a couple of days at Wendell. Weeded peppers nude with Betsy and Dace. Went to sauna party with Mark and Jake, also a goodbye party for Jake [Jake is Mark Kramer's woman-friend — she's leaving to go back to Norway].

Drove for Willet late Sunday afternoon with Betsy [Betsy Cornwoman], and also Franz and Julie who are from Amsterdam, Franz a doctor. They were out at Willet at the very beginning of things — Franz built the bench that we all sit on just outside the front door.

Lots of people here — Bob, friend of Ira's who is a carpenter, Jim and Robin friends of George — Jarlath here, Dianne, Kathy, Claire, Ira, George, and Dana whom I'm back with in the barn.   Couldn't sleep last night — didn't do too much today. While I was away people cleared off the great mess out the back door to find a wooden platform. Veggies not so advanced, though two rows of zucchini are ripe! Picked some. Blackberries out! Picked some with Franz and Julie. Talked about cabin Franz would like to put up. Raining out. Supper's ready. . .

<u>Tuesday, August 9</u>: Didn't do much today — am really confused about dates [most of the Journal not dated, just the days]. Picked some blackberries in the woods — large ones. Peaceful there — saw a Least Flycatcher — also picked a few raspberries.

In the afternoon got into ripping off the el of the barn down — more exactly pulling out the good beams and piling up the no good wood for burning. I am driving the Ford to do this — sort of fun. . .

Then later, late in a cool evening (clear sky — still light enough) drive out to pull out the manure spreader and help George put in the bolts to its front.

Dinner — usual veggies: zucchini, turnip, rhubarb chard and other greens, rice, and apple pie and ice cream after. Then a meeting — Jill sort of running things. Dianne asks about the house — is it really worth saving (we've been winterizing it, putting on 'wacky board'). Yes, Ira says, admitting to language about blowing it up — it is the oldest house in Willet, apparently actually sound. Money as usual is discussed (we're broke). Then, regards the house, Claire tries to put in that whether we work hard to do a first rate job is related to whether we're really going to stay here — whether its our "home". But Jill shuts her right up to make her pitch that we're here for the summer to work and that's it! No necessity for all this analysis — whether or not this is our 'home' is irrelevant. Familiar argument — farm vs commune. Jill kind of blows it here though, which when George tells her same later — well, later. Most of the meeting is about things to do; to put together a vegetable stand, to make a woodshed out the kitchen door, to cut down the great Hemlock in the woods and take to a sawyer, various fields to be plowed, spreading more chicken-shit, the winterizing of the house.

When George tells Jill she blew it, after the meeting, she really blows up—sobbing and throwing things; after calming down a little, she borrows my car to go out with Dianne. Then, putting on a loud record when she returns, another screaming confrontation with George — heard from the barn.

Night beautiful — stars out, milky way clear — cold though, must be in the low forties.

Wednesday, August 10: Have a dream that I am a student at Berkeley or wherever, and involved with a movement, which at the time is into finding exams, etc., and other methods of getting out of doing school work — at one point in the dream see two professors cackling away to each other saying that they will give the students so much work that they won't even have enough energy left to even think about cheating! Took me a little while (telling it to Dana) to catch its relevance to Willet. Like again stayed away from work — went for a long walk with Jim [carpenter friend of Ira's] eating blackberries, finding salamanders under a rock or under a log, talking about philosophy of life. Jim plays the guitar well — is into yoga and some other religious philosophy. Wants to get out of ego trip, which he feels deadens one — is like sleep — to do things out of pride. He comes from South Carolina as does Robin.

Ate some peanut butter and veggies for lunch. Vacillated around all afternoon. Started helping Jill plow the buck-wheat field, but returned to get George and Ira's opinion and found we needed to mow the hay first. George is finishing up fixing the Ford (a hydraulic gasket came out), taking the Ford off the manure spreader. Then Franz came by to invite us to look at cabin site. Had been critical of his first choice, as it was right on the scenic part of the hill. The new site is along the road, and better as it has southern exposure. Looked at old foundation where he could get stone — found huge rhubarb plant. Jill is pissed at me when I finally get back for running out on her.

Helped Franz and Julie a little. Earlier in the day had helped Jarlath get the John Deere ready for plowing, which Betsy finally did as Jarlath went down with Bob to ask about the cutting of the Hemlock. Raining spitfully at the end of the day — supper good.

Thursday, Friday, August 11-12: Went to Ithaca Thursday with Betsy and Franz, Julie, but missed George Sherman. Saw Cornell campus, same [as other campuses] but amazing deep gorges as you approach.

Just finished playing about a dozen games of volleyball. Ira's camp! Eventually got 8 people on a team — couldn't seem to get rotation down. Watched the sun set while playing — clear day. Last night everyone sang and played music, John Anderson coming by from New Mexico. He's the one we cut the cherry tree down for last winter — great tall tree (nice cherry colored wood) which we had great trouble pulling out of the woods — all for making guitars, now all cut up and stored in our barn. Anyway he now plays on a rock and roll band and sang. Ira especially liked the singing.

Night before we had gone to Jerry, music played, George imitating Gene Krupa on drums, Jill dancing with abandon, I'm stoned on 2 beers — play chess with Franz (beat him) and Bob (lose in exciting game which Franz writes down as it takes so long and we finish the next day). Jill seems to have recovered self.

Today is <u>Saturday, August 13th</u> — 1st nice day, Thursday and Friday being rainy — actually played Franz at Clem Casting's house where we go to talk about cabin Franz wants to build partially out of stone. Not much happening, like day after Jerry's everyone is kind of shot, as we didn't get in until 3:30 a.m. or so — brushed teeth affectionately with Jill. Put wacky board on the house, weeded celery patch (like couldn't spend whole day putting up wacky board). Am beat — just drew game with Franz on board carved out of Ira's dining room table.

<u>Sunday / Monday, August 14-15</u>: Too much happening to write much in this book! Beautiful weather, cool at night, cloudless days — hot — but not too. . .

Many visitors Sunday, like George's parents bringing much food — corn, frozen pizza, etc. Strange talking to straight people. Mrs. works for a library where <u>all</u> save maybe a few books ruined by the floods! She suggests we post pretty girls with our veggie stand wagon, "Nothing wrong with a pretty girl!"

Other visitors: Allen and friend from north of here into "biodynamics" such as planting with the moon phases, companion planting; an Amherst couple; George Sherman. John Anderson and Betsy Cornwoman leave which is sad. Betsy, as someone says, has been at it long enough so that work flows — like she does up the manure spreader chains with a torch with a little help from Pete, who's here fixing Clem's 'milk' tractor.

Well, did more wacky board, standing on ladders taking off the old shingles and nails, then measuring, then nailing on the boards (4' by 8'), but usually have to cut them with a saw, sometimes twice.

Interesting game of chess with Ira tonight. We've had nice swims in the creek. Volleyball last night and the one before. More visitors tonight, 3 or 4 friends of Kathy's. Yesterday some Ithaca woman's rights people came and promptly punctured their oil pan. Ira finally fixes it.

Ira, George and I have small meeting — ha! — partly upshot of my conversation with Kathy. She'd like to know better where she stands — possibility of people staying over the winter and buying stock *[Willet is formed as a corporation to facilitate change]*. George is against, and in fact against the hegemony of the girls — Claire, Dana, Kathy — has felt much better with his friends John Anderson, Betsy, Jim, Robin et al. Both sides clear enough — girls anti visitors really, Claire saying she won't cook for them, Kathy wanting a close community of a few, all a little insecure about their position — maybe its just George and Ira's farm. Dana has declared the barn a dormitory and has moved to the attic, several days back in fact. I woke up after Jerry's party to find George sleeping next to me! Since then have been sleeping alone up there, Jim and Robin and Claire sleeping in other sections. For me, still feel unsettled, not quite my place. . .

Tuesday, Wednesday August 17, 18: Another, well not quite — a haze — but otherwise clear. Sat around and finally got started on a little wacky board, when the great day arrived! For, through *[George]* calling our 'friend' Dr. Hoffman in Syracuse (a health doctor freak who last year *[told us]* he got a real lift from eating our veggies), who knows well the Pres of C & D Groceries (a big supermarket up here), *[he]* got us a contract for 1,000 bunches (5 to 8 depending on size) of white radishes!! 11¢ a bunch—$110! So, after a sort of meeting in the kitchen led by Dianne, we all set forth to picking white radishes in our mixed veggie patch, also setting up a big washing and packaging operation.

LABELS WE DREW

A page of the Journal follows with one the label drawings! Journal got wet in Willet bookcase.

Tuesday & wednesday —
Another, well not quite - a haze - but otherwise clear - sat around & finally got started on a little wacky board when the great day of the

the great white radish

organically grown
and distributed by

willet produce inc.

arrived! For through calling our 'friend' Dr. Hoffman in Syracuse (a health Doctor freak who last year got a real lift from eating our vegy's) who knows well the Pres of C+D groceries (a big supermarket up there) got us a contract for 1000 bunches (5 to 8 depending on size) of white radishes!! So after a sort of meeting in the kitchen led by Dianne we all set forth to picking white radishes in our mixed vegy patch) & inaddition setting up a big washing and packaging operation @ 11¢ a bunch

None of the labels we drew got used — we managed to finish a little after sunset with one half a box to go! Played some more chess. . .

Today, Wednesday (8/16) everyone lazed around mostly after yesterday. Bob and Jill got up early to take the radishes to Syracuse; Jarlath took the second trip in the Datsun. Manager couldn't pay us our money (computer troubles), and was taken a-back by our delivery, "White radishes?? Who's going to buy white radishes?? I've been in this business forty years," etc.   Went around with George — found a little corn to pick, looked at the melons and peppers and tomatoes. Some peppers ripe including a yellow variety which, depending, is sweet or hot!

Dotty Horacks *[a local]* comes up with her father who had raised 300 acres of vegetables with just two other people on Long Island! Dotty loudmouths Ira into going out into the field, "or I'll put a corn cob up your ass!" *[to pick some corn]*. The old man knows about black radishes, which are a mystery to us. Jarlath and I go down to their house bringing corn as that is what they specially wanted. Big scene, Jim Horacks, who has left his eight hour job to go into business with Clem (contracting), the parents (much energy, tales of farming on Long Island), little Billy and 5 or 6 other children running back and forth — guessing game goes on of all our ages, and Dotty feeds us food — beer, shrimp macaroni, rice pudding (not too good). Then Jarlath and I go swimming, everyone down there.

Much talk this night — Kathy made joke of it last night "constant comment" (tea) — over kitchen duties this time, directed towards Ira and George, also Jill, for never doing any kitchen work. Actually Julie is doing most of it — good stuff — like pudding last night with coconut and blackberries, millet, veggies (including cooked white radishes — not-so-good). Talk goes on to whole problem of George's rejection of the women, and his chauvinism. Much trouble results, I think, from Betsy's saying she was leaving because of hostile vibes from the women. Guess upshot of all talk is that the women will ride it out, and confront without confronting (that is talk to George and do projects with him). Jim says I am peacemaker. Robin, Claire and I all talk till really late, reading early pages out of this journal — amazing!

Thursday, Friday August 17, 18: Days slide into one another — rain one day — went for long walk, saw some deer. Then hot sun again — picked vegetables for Belly of the Whale, a Binghamton organic restaurant and store — radishes (mostly red), zucchini, etc. In the afternoon helped Franz with this cabin he's building, all with joints so that few nails used, the beams coming from the old el of the barn that we tore down, also the ruined house on the hill.

TALK. Receive an amazing riff from Jill — she had gone down to the Beaver with George and Dianne and was a little drunk. George told her of my comment as she drove off on the radish day, "Well, there goes our foreman." So, with flashing eyes, and manic, she confronts me and denies it, "Absolutely untrue! — Show me an example," etc. I'm equivocating, tongue tied, unmanic. She goes on to give philosophy — she has only a few friends "I can only give myself to a few people — I only want to help George and Ira," etc. She confesses to being a "hard ass" — "After all I was once a 'hood'."

Almost return to the Beaver with Jill (she collects Jarlath). Are not Jill, Dianne, George, Jarlath from the 50s? Dianne always has such a sweet smile, acts like a sorority queen, always confident. George with all his women. Jarlath seems like a beatnik — a loner — has that aspect — can communicate with the locals while someone like Kathy I think can't (nor Claire).

Next night George gives me whole riff — not liking Kathy, for instead of accepting Willet as it is she is trying to change it. True to a certain extent, but — I don't know. He's all against Claire — says she claims to be VW mechanic, and then doesn't know what a 'head' is. Well, Claire does have a certain trying to prove herself thing for sure, but I can't think she ever said she is a VW mechanic.

I'm baffled and in the middle here. What's embarrassing is the fact that Jill and Dianne seem to really like me, and I can't reciprocate, not without trying to be into a 50s thing, which I wasn't any good at anyway — liquor, dirty jokes, secrets, intense private relations, no self consciousness. . . George I can take better as besides charm and enthusiasm he has real talent (farming, music) — a lot like brother George. — Not that I'm so far into 70s consciousness — rather 'hip' consciousness.

Lets see — things: Ira goes to N. Y. with Franz and Julie. Jarlath leaves with Kathy while I'm talking with George. Have various talks with Franz [before he leaves]. He feels the women here are very selfish, unsharing, bitchy in short. Julie, your European woman, <u>has</u> without least complaint, and with enthusiasm done all this cooking — main courses, breads (one loaf with cheese in the middle), etc., besides doing all this weeding in the garden (which no one else has touched), and helped Franz with his cabin. Kathy in contrast (spoiled brat that she is) has made a terrific fuss about the kitchen (fact that Ira and George never do anything nor Jill and Dianne, though in fact Kathy rarely does anything (not that much anyway), and will often cook something just for herself, and she is possessive — i.e. won't let Julie ride her horse. Woman's lib hasn't reached Holland. Have long talk with Dana about all this, and with Robin and Claire. Don't get to sleep until 3 a.m. or so. Tell them I will leave next season — won't put my body where my money is!

Ira's fatal flaw we agree is violence and violent language, but we agree he's much improved, mellower, less upset, etc. since or because of his relationship with Kathy.

George says opposite — complains they bitch at each other like a married couple — they do somewhat.

Veggies actually ripening — stand will open in a few days — Claire and Robin building it — will resemble a covered wagon — from an old wagon George found in the barn. Dana and I weed and thin half a row of our mixed veggies — takes easily two hours, and then takes practically as long to sort and wash (beet greens, rhubarb chard, radishes). There must be 25 or 30 such rows. Some of the peppers are ripe. We eat good corn first time today!

Morning sun. George is sitting across the dining room table from me doing up a sign advertising the stand. He and Dianne went to this biodynamic conference in Spring Valley, New York, but hitched back same day — boring.

Didn't do much today. Picked woods blackberries this morning (amazingly prolific) but then man who ordered them doesn't come by. Jim found some apple and pear trees on our land — delicious little round pears. Dana made an apple and blackberry pie last night.

Shall I do a poster? Think m.b. not.

FRESH VEGETABLE WAGON FROM WILLET OPENS AUGUST 19TH
ORGANIC / NO PESTICIDES / NO CHEMICALS
Drawings of radish, corn, tomato, summer squash.
TOMKIN'S STREET EXTENSION, CORTLAND, N.Y.

<u>Monday, Tuesday, Wednesday, August 19, 20, 21</u>: STAND OPENS — we spend most of Monday night sewing together the canvas and otherwise getting it ready. Sewed from perhaps 10 until 2 so that my back got sore. Dianne stayed up all night making signs — fancy design with vegetables looking more like something for a boutique than our down to-earth-stand. Our stand is sort of a covered wagon, only the wagon is really small, so with flaps up and out it really looks funny. But it is nice — an ancient wagon, bins for the veggies and shade for them.

Quite a trip that, getting up really early after this late night to pick — lettuce, beet greens, rhubarb chard, few radishes, corn, peppers, zucchini, then washing, then Jill and I got it together to be an advance party to the stand to sell out of the Datsun until our great covered wagon should be ready. Which we did, sort of sprawled around as we'd been up so late, selling the veggies to our mostly fancy customers (Cadillacs!), and a few young people. Then finally the dump truck arrives with the stand, canvas flapping in the wind. Much bustle, including visit from Town clerk, an ancient, well old, politician, "Who's in charge here?" To which no one answers, so he speaks into the air about how we're illegal, how ugly we are — he's going to close us down by noon tomorrow, with neighbors across the street gesticulating and yelling, "They don't pay taxes — I didn't purchase this property to look across at these (hippies)." But in the end, next day. . .

Too much violence in this place! Like *[another time than just now]* George fucking Dianne (turns out it was Franz and Julie) upstairs so mattress is creaking like crazy, and Jarlath just hit me in the ass — they were drinking and dancing in the next room while Franz and I were playing chess, so that I came sort of close to hitting him. And the day before yesterday I really shocked Jim by throwing stones at Mandarin the puppy for barking at me as I came across the field, and shocked myself as well when I thought of it (sending him howling off as I hit him from some 30 or 40 feet).

I really don't like just listening to music and getting stoned — the only reason I didn't hit Jarlath — well I guess its obvious. He and Kathy have both come back as well as Ira and Franz and Julie. Claire and Robin have left. I am more than ready to split this place, but I guess I'll stay over Labor Day weekend. Too many people in this little house for sure.

<u>August 22nd</u>, Thursday afternoon — as the expression goes I'm freaked! Did nothing all day (beautiful day) save pick a little corn and sell a few veggies to people who come up *[we have sign down on the main road]*. Turns out other people are too, which Jill and Ira call a crisis in leadership — no one really working. They plan to have meetings every morning and night, get up at 6, and henceforth run a tight ship! Undoubtedly they're right. There is much to do — mostly harvest — but importantly spreading chicken manure and preparing the fields, and additionally preparing for winter — freezing, cutting wood, putting up wacky board and so on.

<u>August 23, Friday</u>: Zucchinis here! Started chicken shit with Kathy and Jarlath. I'm taking off though — spending Sunday and hopefully Monday with Carey and Nadia McIntosh (Carey teaches at Rochester Univ.), and then Monday night or Tuesday am setting forth for Cambridge probably to stay at least 5 days. . .

<u>August 24-25 Sat Sun</u>: Do visit Carey and Nadia — strange — take a shower and read the N. Y. Times and the New Yorker. Carey looks exactly the same, his hair not an inch longer, but his kids hair is long and blond — Rustin and Nathaniel quite beautiful, 6 and 8 or something like that. Found him *[Carey]* up in a big apple tree in his back yard *[pruning]* — no power tools does he have. Nadia makes home-made bread — uses potatoes and grains. We go out to their cabin in the woods *[Gennessee River & canyon]*. We cook up the corn I brought along — good! — and get into building a porch (finding logs for beams). Not a bad place, only lumbered *[second growth woods]*. It's a grey occasionally drizzly day. Weirdly the railroad goes nearby *[you hear the trains]*.

<u>August 26-31 Mon-Sat:</u> *[Trip to Cambridge]:* Am in Colrain waiting for Mark Kramer. He's just arrived and demands my attention, this being written about two weeks later. Lets see, Mark talks me into spending the night. He who originally urged me to live in the country is going to lease my apartment in Cambridge! Spent some time at Wendell — beautiful garden — help Betsy pick pod peas and peppers, their pepper plants being about twice as luxurious and bountiful as ours. Have more-or-less decided to spend the winter at Wendell, to sleep in Ira's cabin. Keller and Betsy both glad! Sell a bushel of peppers for goods at Corners of the Mouth *[Cambridge].*

Back in Cambridge see people in my building. More-or-less arranged to have Peter Burns (leather maker) run the building for me at half rent. Talk to Craig *[Ace]* — gives me book on the rise of fascism in Germany after WW 1. Chapter on back-to-nature, early myths, anti business/bureaucracy — German kids like present hippies. Analogous?? Craig thinks so!

Go out to Borderland and am again attracted to it — a mink splashes across stream, and feel mission to be involved in its becoming a park. Spend night at the Ericsons. Daughter Ann sends me a poem *[see below].* But for all that Borderland is beautiful, guess I should stay away — its now in the suburbs and one would have to live what I call a city life — hustle in other words, and besides — family! Best stick to the spirit of raid we did on the farm implements *[Ford tractor].* So I wrote Ginny Reusch *[Friends of Borderland Pres.]* which typed while I was at Steve and Beth's in Acton, where I spent 4 or 5 hours Saturday, among other things playing croquet! I also wrote Betsy that I wished I might spend harvest at Wendell, especially if I'm going to spend the winter there, but, well, guess I must harvest the veggies we planted this spring in this chaotic place. But beautiful *[written later]* sat in cut over corn field yesterday talking with George, with sun out and a pair of Cooper's Hawks circling — big sky — reminds me of out West — definitely not "home".

In harvesting panic, completely organic, how does your garden grow?
With tomatoes and beans - and no picking machines - and radishes all in a row.

September & October

<u>September 1-2 Sun-Mon:</u> Lets see — left Steve and Beth late on Saturday, 5 or so, got to Wendell in a couple of hours. Everyone just taking off, Franz and Julie, etc. Montague has just been raided! Steve and Tony arrested for dope — local cops (not Feds). Wendell freaked into going out and pulling all their marijuana plants — some 7 feet tall taking two to pull them *[took part].* Not yet flowered — beautiful plants — planted in amongst the corn.

Pick up George Sherman and drive up to Vermont to pick up Shelley *[who had worked for me at Conservation Law]* who wanted to spend a week out at Willet, and then to Willet starting out at around 10:45 p.m. Got arrested on way for speeding. Got to Willet around 4:15 a.m. to find George and friend of his (Andy) still up! Jill and Dianne had just left for N.Y. with truckful of corn and veggies, Ira also same day!

September 3, Tuesday: Turns out we didn't end up having meetings or anything — Jill acknowledges she forgot we are to have fun, but people do start getting up earlier (7 or 7:30). Spend day with Jarlath at the stand — manage to trade zucchinis to faculty student association at Cortland University for promised beet greens and deliver them *[beet greens promised, zucchinis delivered]*.

Jarlath has bought this white horse, nice horse, friendlier than Enterprise—who is ecstatic to have horse companion — muzzles him, and then they cavort in the field. The white horse runs away, and Jarlath, finally finding him, rides him back fording the river twice, once where the horse has to swim! Jarlath goes to Rod and Donna's church with purpose to find a pair of crutches as he stepped on two deep nails and wrenches his neck in the bargain. Describes it as quite the occasion, the minister's wife most energetic, reading the Bible, etc., everyone testifying, everyone shaking his hand.

Jarlath, Jill, Ira and Kathy are all mixed up in sexual square, and apparently false VD test showing positive (Kathy) sends them all running to the Cortland health clinic. Lets see, Ira sleeps with Kathy, and Jill with Jarlath, and on Jarlath's trip to Mass., Kathy seduces him in Ira's cabin at Wendell, thus the connection between the four, Kathy bringing the news back too late for J and J. But anyway turns out just to have been a scare.

Jarlath and I sell out early (Labor Day) and come back to share French fries with Kathy and Dana at Whelan's, then on coming up the hill we pick up bicyclist who has been attracted by my Fresh Veggies sign. We all get into a zucchini picking evening, including Dan from Willet with girl friend and bicyclist, about 14 of us, another Arabian friend of George's having arrived. We're putting the zucchinis into bags and then into the (clean) manure spreader behind the Deere.

September 4 - 8 Wed - Sun: Kathy reads this Journal! So I guess I'd better hide it from now on. Doesn't like it at all my saying she 'seduced' Jarlath — she also accuses me of blanding it out—being too bland, also making things sound like Peyton Place, etc. Fuck! Actually haven't talked to Kathy, and maybe I should, she's just left for Massachusetts for five days.

Feel strange, as though summer is over and its time to end vacation and start 'work'. Instead we have quite a long ways to go on this harvest. Spent most of the day fishing with Andy — no catches.

Was nice having Shelley up for the week. She is game — we all went together bringing veggies to an organic store in Syracuse, and then afterwards selling at the farmers' market in Syracuse *[like Haymarket]* — nice bustle of people, farmers, I'm shouting out "organic corn here, 60¢!" and towards the end 50¢ *[a dozen]*. We had arrived quite late. . .

Ira and Jill have trouble selling their produce *[at the Cortland stand]*. In fact they come back with 8 crates of unsold corn.

We have amazing harvest Friday — beautiful day — great huge beets, nice chard, beautiful Chinese cabbages, lots of peppers, cucumbers, the perennial zucchini! Go down to New York City with Hamish — long trip in the Datsun pick-up stopping both ways with Ira's relatives in Monticello — strange driving all around New York City delivering veggies — some people quite receptive — guy cracks open watermelon and we all try it (they're getting ripe, and we found one cantaloupe), and feeds around a hot pepper. Another guy bargains us down in price — places: *World Health Center, Greenhouse, Great Organics, Back on the Farm Restaurant, Earth something*, that last being phony place!

People: Jill and Dianne have left — some bitter feelings — partly due to frustrating trip to N.Y. where among other things they're ripped off $60 — but more out of tenseness. Ira has sort of withdrawn his approval of Jill — decided to cool it with her which Jill interprets as total rejection! Things are a little better now — in fact I dreamt they smiled at one another. Also they plan to get jobs so as they can go to Europe.

Jarlath left and still not back — sent us postcard which mostly named everybody!

Kathy is in Mass., taking along Dana who is talking of wintering on the Cape.

Franz and Julie came and left. Jim came back and is staying until Wednesday, when he leaves for Afghanistan etc. As noted Hamish is back from his trans-country trek, which he hasn't said much about. Jill and Dianne back for weekend. Julie and Twink here, guests of Claire. We—George, Ira, Hamish and I—are going to organic farm meeting tomorrow early.

Week of Sept 9 - 16 *[hard to keep track of the dates]*— Really cold night — beautiful moon night before — FROST — nothing really hurt — zucchini has blackened leaves. Conference interesting really — possibility of cooperating with other organic farmers around. Did a lot of picking today both for N.Y. and organic store in Cortland. Spread manure this afternoon. Yesterday awful and rainy. Picked some apples in the afternoon *[old orchard on the farm]*.

Lets see — Claire has left for Mass. and long trip west, planning to farm next summer with good friends near Potsdam, New York, a little bitter I guess — both George and Ira feel she exaggerated her knowledge (i.e. woman's lib). Jim leaves. Kathy and Dana come back bringing Jarlath. They meet of all things near Central Square and spend some time at my Cambridge building. Ace breaks into my apartment as his master key doesn't work, so Kathy can have a place to stay. Andy comes back from Penn. for a few days, and Bob Koorse due in with Jim's van.

This is now Friday night, the above written Sunday night. Routine of working in the fields, and minor picking — zucchini for Grand Union. Planted some winter wheat in one field with 19th century grain drill, which on last turn fell into several pieces!

September 17 - October 1: Yesterday Ira and I went on tour to visit other farms to talk of cooperative arrangements (markets, equipment, freight car load of rock phosphate, etc.). One farm is manned by N.Y.C. Germans — river flat land — sun finally came out while we were there — much tomatoes, cabbage, etc., which we are to try to sell for them. Stopped at Dawes Hill — amazing again what careful gardening will do, like zucchini plants 3 times as big as ours, 16 pound cabbage heads, beautiful cauliflower, etc.

Colors changing out here — beautiful maples here and there, the old field next to the melons dotted with yellow hawthorns. Today a bunch of girls came by from some Penn. college a la Andy and got stuck here for the night due to flat tires — showed them around. Before had picked scallions, beets and zucchini for Ithaca Co-op run. Had usual amazing dinner — freshly baked bread (and sweet roll of extra dough) stuffed peppers (lentils, etc.), enormous salad (lettuce, cukes, tomatoes, Chinese and regular cabbage), good cauliflower, corn-on-the-cob, small boiled potatoes, and last sort of an apple dish from Hamish. Ira and I froze two bags of broccoli which didn't quite get cooked, and Hamish and I had frozen 12 half gallons of zucchini a few days back.

Frost! Ira at first said everything gone — "guess we can pack it up"! But as the sun came out it turned out that, ice everywhere to the contrary, most of the plants were OK, even maybe the melons which were the hardest hit. So we spent the whole day picking for the New York trip (this is Sunday). Picked mostly carrots — hard to extract the soil so compacted, and beets, and finally (more!) zucchini with Jarlath — into the night. Whole cooperative venture with other farmers falls through as we have to drive to New York, Ira leaving at three in the morning!

Not much doing today Monday. Froze some beets and chard (over picked). Am ready to go back, tho' suppose will stay around 'till weekend. Made spaghetti sauce with Kathy.

<u>Early October</u>: Am back in Cambridge, and this being Thursday have been away from Willet for a while — not so much further enlightened — read some of this to Eleanor *[friend]* a lot of days say how much we sat around, spaced around, but then quite a lot seems to get done, not truly tho' in proportion of time spent. Anyway, I'm not sure I can reconstruct. I left on a rainy Friday, no Saturday. We didn't do a Wednesday pick, so I left before the weekend effort. People did get it together to prepare a "care" package for my mother as interest on her loan so to speak *[delivered to her N.Y. apartment]*, and I learned from her that a freeze had really hit Willet so as to, among other things, destroy $500 worth of melons.

Things pretty slow that last week with much discussion of the future. Jarlath is really the only one who really wants to stay — to see the other end of the season, the Spring! He's gotten to know half the town through his horse, whom he calls "White Horse," quite a neat nag really, ghostly on moonlit nights. He has a funny habit of laying down, but full of energy and go once you get on him, and wants to do nothing else but gallop. I finally actually went for a ride, only on Enterprise, a little tough as uncomfortable for sure (am bareback as Jarlath is on White Horse). Enterprise is stubborn and keeps stopping. We finally get into a gallop going up the second hill, the colors really spectacular, fiery red and yellow and orange — all really in the last few days.

Lets see, finally did a testing program (pretty skimpy) on our tomatoes and peppers — all the different varieties, with Hamish picking each variety noting how prolific the plant is. Then, the next day, tasting everything. Ira, George and I think Jill were sitting there when started tasting, all clapped for the taste of, I think, Ponderosa tomato, as if we were at an agricultural fair. One thing we discovered was that one of the ordinary green peppers was hot — must have cross-pollinated! The other project we did was to count the Chinese cabbages — we figured approximately 200 ripe, 1,000 getting there (wonder how the freeze affected them). . .

Well, much talk — future of Willet. Came to a head in planning for next year, specifically in applying for a disaster Government loan (which you can keep). For Ira's figures come out to show that we'll have to spend ten thousand (!): $2,800 on the mortgage, and going on our past figures and projecting (we spent $1,400 on gas this year!). So, as it is really difficult to gross $10 thousand selling vegetables (we'll be lucky to gross 5000 this year), and as neither George or Ira are quite into it — into putting all out (as among other things they're at odds with one another), talk has come around (in fact initiated by Ira) to selling Willet again, first some acreage (like the second hill including some of the north woods in one approx. 100 acre parcel, the old orchard, plus most of the buckwheat field and south woods), which possibly could bring back enough money to repay/retire the mortgage. A possible prospect is David Beach, Amherst friend of Ira's and George who deals in dope and wants a hide-away (presumably not to grow dope) and has money! Well, but soon coming around to either selling the whole farm, or essentially keeping it as an investment for a few years, me and Ira's stepfather keeping up the mortgage (I offered to), which would have added advantage of giving us further time to think about the whole thing.

Naturally I've mixed emotions, having sublet my Cambridge apartment to Mark Kramer, and I've spent so much time here, and not at Wendell where supposedly I'm to move — nice there, Ira's cabin neat to wake up in to look outside to see a pine tree — saw Blue Jay flash by, like nestled in a valley instead of standing so starkly on top of a hill in such boonies! I even feel like its <u>my</u> place, and I would like to spend the winter there. Fuck, I know better, best forget and settle where there is more tradition and character and history and culture! No — Yes —

<u>Late October</u>: Should I write further in this Journal? Am back here — first stopped at Steve and Beth's in Acton, Patrick and Monica there, talk of planning *[we were all students at UMass Amherst in Environmental Planning]*. Then stopped by Wendell and Montague — spent most of the day putting up a side of a house with Jim Aaron in charge! Kind of neat. Spent night with Claire Van Pesky. Went to John Moore's service, a classics teacher from Amherst College, people's spoken memories really boring. *[I never took Latin, but became his friend, a special man]*. Before that went to *[cousin]* Polly and Nat's wedding out at the *Cape [Polly's father my Uncle Calvin, who became President of Amherst]*.

Drove out Monday, October 16th, now its Friday, October 20th, early winter! Drove along Route 20 through great snow squalls, windy, great clouds. Got down to 12 degrees last night. Went walking up the hill the night before last, the dusting of snow bright in the moon. Saw a skunk, its tail up over its back, moving with dignity.

Ira, George, Dana, Kathy, Bobby (came back at last with Jim's van), Jarlath here. Jarlath has sold White Horse — sad — to a horse dealer who in a way talked him out of it. We had talked at length about riding White Horse all the way to Vermont where Joannie, his girl firend, lived, stopping by farmer's houses, etc., but that was a fantasy!

We went out to harvest potatoes the next day with the potato picker, but it turns out whole crop is a bust — riddled with wire worms!! *[We had planted a whole field of potatoes! Later I heard that that's the risk you take if you plant potatoes in an old field]*.

Take long walk with Dianne. Turns out deal is that George is going to sell out — money from David Beach to pay off Dick, who still has $4,000 outstanding, and Jay, George's Arabian friend, who has another $4,000, and then George himself, about $5,000, but I think George will stick it out. He's more up and down than Ira.

Jarlath leaves. Jill and Dianne come and go.

David and Elaine Beach arrive to save us! To buy 100 acres and more for $20,000. We all spent some time today pulling up back plastic in the graveyard that is the melon field — all these frozen melons!

Usual feast for dinner! Still have beets, carrots, Chinese cabbage, ordinary cabbage from the kitchen garden. Did a little fire wood with Bobby. . .

Today is Friday *[October 27th?]* — guess last entry was Sunday — am not sure. Since then drove all the way down to New York City to collect money from David Beach, consult a lawyer and the like — much a do about how to hide the money. We're paid $10,000 in cash yet! Go around *[Willet and Cincinnatus]* and pay all our bills, McKee's and the S & D in cash, couple of thousand in the bank, part to pay off some of the mortgage. Pearl Crittendon *[who sold us the farm]* says she'll give us a release so we can sell the land (release from the mortgage) though at the moment she's concerned about the timber rights. But her daughter, who signs everything, knows better — plenty of equity left, 250 acres and only $24,000 left to pay. They were sympathetic, wanting us to make it.

Has been cold and rainy, but today and yesterday quite beautiful — went for a long walk yesterday. Mowed down some corn stalks today with the Ford — nice to be on a tractor again.

George left today for Philadelphia — to stay with Dianne. We all think he should do the night club circuit *[play the drums and be a comedian]*. Hence Ira, Kathy and me here, Dana to return after the weekend I guess.

Sunday *[10/29?]* — Grey and rain both yesterday and today, but at least not cold; picked beets before breakfast for a lady at the Cincinnatus post office who wants to pickle them — got block of stamps in return. Ira, Kathy and I went driving, first to Triangle thrift shop, Ira to get picture frame for his mother, then to drugstore in Greene to have some home-made pie (had some popcorn at Triangle), then to junk yard to find a spring for Kathy's car which had broken. Came back here, but had to go back out to collect my papers which had left when I got the eggs, and went by a store to buy some peanut butter, cheese and cider. Played a Spaasky / Fischer game with Ira, eating practically everything had just bought — it's a symbol of our (my) sickness that we eat so much — I can't stop, no governor of civilization to stop me, no inspiration for discipline or stuff I want to do — hence, among other things thinking of returning to the city and calling it a day re communal life! Back to playing tennis, which I'm good at — dreamt about same last night, playing these amazing strokes with this girl, Uncle Paschall looking on.

Susan, Jill's cousin comes to visit with three guys from around Wilkes-Barre, an analogue of Jill, same age, looks a little like her and carries herself in much the same manner — she's thin, stands erect, smokes, but she has love or whatever it is, she smiles — hasn't the paranoia of Jill. Have come to think that much of divisiveness around here stems from Jill (like George is too easy-going to have been so anti-Claire), and she is far too uptight in her possessiveness of this place. But it isn't right to put the blame on her for sure!

Anyway, among other things Clem Castings came by and told his version of the happenings the evening Jill claimed he tried to make her, semi-rape her, which of course entirely different — that he was merely fooling around with her, and in fact carried her down the hill from her tent on his shoulders. I'm inclined to believe him, for one thing did confuse me was that if they'd had all these bad vibes, how could Clem have been so casual, etc., for he behaved (then) as though nothing had happened! Clem told of some of the winter goings-on, everyone completely drunk, staying up all night, having snow fights, Jill throwing an ax, everyone down at the Beaver.

Susan described being into the area where she lives — they had had to move to their country place because of the floods. She worked for the local paper, taught horse-back riding, has been learning how to cook. She's anti-religion regarding same as a crutch — one of her friends is into yoga, etc.

[Arrow from earlier paragraph]: But no doubt Jill had by then ceased to flirt, and there's a side to her story. Talked with Kathy and Ira — we all go to the movies — some Audrey Hepburn mystery at Cortland State College, and Sunday ice cream afterwards.

Later talked with Jim Ord *[who came by]*. He felt there was a real energy and spirit last year which dissipated towards the end — true —. He feels it was George who fucked things up in the end with his romantic communal bullshit! In their original conception Willet was going to more of a cooperative enterprise, people to live in separate houses, etc. He also felt George kind of went crazy over the winter (he *[George]* felt you had to spend the winter in a place to really get into it!), but that he went over to Jerry Skaags house too much and got into the anti-local paranoia. We agree it's not so easy to move to the country as you bring all your old baggage with you! (I myself kind of regret I didn't enter into the local scene more, like Jarlath).

We get a letter from Jim — he and Robin got caught red-handed in Afghanistan! And are now residing in jail, described by an article we had read in the N.Y. Times a week before as the worst jail in the World! (From their letter, though, it doesn't sound so bad). Trouble is their fine could be as high as $1,800 a piece, and a day in jail only relieves 75¢ of the fine!

A little weird here animal-wise as Enterprise took off, and Corn Dog too, the latter having mouthed up two of the kittens, practically killing one, but both showed up, and guess kitten will make it. — Nope, died the next day —.

Kathy and Ira leave early a.m. — long discussion back and forth night before, Kathy uptight about having to live in Ira's territory of Wendell, etc., her deal of going to her parents' place in Braintree to sell her horse at leisure having fallen through. Ira as usual makes little of it — he always pretends the environment means little to him. We point out obviously it does as witness his hostile behavior in the early part of the summer. . . .

So I'm alone out here! Am sitting here, half shivering in front of the stove in the kitchen, having just had a snack, listening to T.V. Had found out, happily, that the building in Cambridge is OK, Peter having gotten up his $200, and insurance straightened out. — Had supper at the Beaver watching the news. Stopped in at the Hovack's and Clem Castings playing a few games of chess with Cheryl.

In the morning picked various veggies for our landlady, Pearl Crittenden and family, carrots mainly plus some onions, broccoli, cabbage etc., beets for George and Sybil at the Beaver, a few carrots and onions for the Willet post office lady, and some carrots and Chinese cabbage for the Belly of the Whale in Binghamton. Also took some veggies to the health food store in Cortland, the latter in trade for cider and soy sauce. Got some new copies of the aerial view of the farm to assist in trying to do land sale project. This afternoon cut some corn stalks.

HALLOWEEN — Drove all the way to Binghamton in Jim's van, bringing along Corn Dog who licks my face every 5 or 10 minutes or so — for all her stupidity nice to have around. Tried a little home-made bread and spread at the Belly, delivering the veggies — traded for brown rice, peanut butter, figs, etc. Talked with Frank *[the owner]*. Couldn't get people motivated to come out to Willet this year, maybe next!

Sat with Dottie (Pearl) quite a while *[bringing carrots, etc.]*. They were all into Halloween, having made all these cookies with faces, candied apples and cup cakes of which sampled some of the latter. Their children came back from school, one whining I guess from being hassled on the school bus, but with an Excedrin and some affection she seemed to recover. All are going to get dressed up, the littlest one as Little Black Sambo!

Spend most of (some of) the evening with Dan Mullins in town giving out gum, also apples, to all these children in their plastic Halloween costumes. Talked about Willet — everyone on ego trip up here for sure we agree *[ourselves?]* — big vegetable farmers, political women, etc. Looks like things will be more realistic now. Ironically enough, of course, money will now come from selling real estate — and dope money!

Come back up the hill to be greeted by George with shot gun (!)—a la Jerry. He has had his hair cut, sports jacket on — has an apartment in suburban Philadelphia with Dianne. Feels strange, but he may get a job outdoors with another Amherst guy he contacted.

Am sitting by the fire, late Wednesday afternoon — gathering darkness, threatening skies — snow?! Spent most of the day picking Chinese cabbage with George, having called up Village Market in Boyertown — some 27 crates we picked, about 250-300 cabbages. . . .

Entry by Ira: AT THIS TIME MR. PLIMPTON (O.A.) FELL FROM A LADDER AND FRACTURED HIS ANKLE. FORTUNATELY HIS HEAD WAS SPARED.

IRA! That's the truth — I'm sitting here in Cortland Hospital waiting to get out, having had my ankle operated on, and now in a cast. Was putting up storm windows (plastic). Of course put the ladder in a crazy position on a smooth rock and at too much an angle. Fell only about 12 feet, but that was enough! A piece of the big leg bone which forms the mortise for the ankle was broken off, and the doctor had to screw it back on. 52 minutes he said the whole thing took, the day of the operation being a complete blank. Five weeks in a cast, then three weeks on a walking cast.

I think this all must have happened at least a few days after the last entry, Halloween. Ira wrote me later (recently) the doctor's name was Dr. Butcher! Only occasionally on damp days can I slightly feel the screw in my leg, no problem to walk and run. The operation cost $5,000 which I paid for by check, having no health insurance. . . .

Note: Much later in time, 2011, when I sent word to my 1950 Amherst Classmates about the project to write this account of my year at Willet, a classmate who lived near Cortland, New York, Stew Vernooy, wrote me that his best friend Dr. George Mauler had performed the operation, and that he had come to the hospital to visit me! He said I seemed really out of it, perhaps from pain killers, and I myself have no memory of it. As you may see Ira's memory was a little off, but close!

Postscript
— 1973 Season

Crutches! Perhaps Ira gave me a ride back to Cambridge, I can't remember. I do remember traveling with my mother to Nashville, Tenn. to attend my cousin's wedding, still on crutches. We went to the symphony there, impressive in that both the audience and the orchestra were integrated both by color and gender! My winter, as I remember it, was occupied by finishing up the rehab of 246 - 250 Brookline Street, Cambridge. Ira rented the apartment below me to go to Harvard Law School, where he became one of Prof. Lawrence Tribe's Interns. Jill and Diane came to live in my front room for a few months—summer school?? Another Wendell Commune couple moved in with me for a while, the one a good portrait painter, who learned how to butcher the steers they raised at Wendell! Broke, they chose to move to Cambridge and sell their bodies, for they were both very personable and very handsome!

   Willet Produce farm still operated on a reduced scale that next season. Jarlath, whom I'd introduced to the farm, became its principal, and in fact a number of people from Brookline Street started journeying out there. Jim Grossi took the black and white photographs herein. Paul Karapetian, Lori Wische, Jim Moyaliyak, Joe O'Rourke, Ray McManus, Alice Grossman all stayed for a couple of weeks up to several months. Follows some of their descriptions of their time there! But first a detail from the 1973 season — I did return for a couple of weeks that year, and the letter following refers to an event that happened just before I journeyed out there. The letter never got sent:

Dear Governor Rockefeller,   July, 1973

We are writing you to protest an invasion of our civil rights by the New York State police, namely, that on Wednesday, July ___, they flew over our farm with a helicopter making three or four passes at no more than 50 feet above the ground looking at us with binoculars, etc., and then finally landing on the top of a hill on our farm near one of the shelters. We called up the State police, but they said it was perfectly legal.

71

(At that time we didn't know about the landing on the hill as it is a ways from the main house where we live — a neighboring farmer reported it).

If it is legal, 1984 has arrived. The constitutional right against search and seizure was violated. No more blatant disregard of the basic right of privacy can be imagined than the blasting noise of this helicopter wheeling just over the roof tops of the house and barn! I suppose they came to harass us because we have long hair and farm communally, and to look for marijuana!? I don't know. And people wonder why there is violence in our land!

As citizens of the State of New York and farmers of organic vegetables in Willet New York, we petition that you cease this practice of helicopter spying on your citizenry, and prosecute the New York state police officers involved in this illegal 'raid' on our farm.

Respectfully yours,

Oakes & Jim Mihaliak with the cows
— photo by Jim Grossi.

Brookline Street Crowd Tales

*As mentioned people from Brookline Street came to live
on the farm — their tales! First an account by Jim Grossi,
whose photographs grace this volume, dated 8/18/08:*

WILLET PRODUCE FARM VISITS

I made several visits to the farm on Mooney Hill Rd in Willet, N.Y. during the
mid seventies. I came to know about Willet through "the Brookline St. boys," Ray
McManus, Paul Karapetian, and of course Oakes, who was one of the owners of the
farm. Oakes invited me to go for a visit and out I went. I remember driving there in
my old Ford Falcon station wagon, a car that could get you there or leave you cursing by
the side of the road. Luckily, she proved her worthiness and got me there without any
issues.

The ride there from Boston seemed to take forever, winding through two lane
highways passing open fields heavy with fog. When I finally got to the town of Willet,
I passed through the smallest "center of town" I had ever seen. It consisted of a gas
station/general store on one corner, a ball field, a post office and diagonally opposite
that, across from the PO was the *Brown Beaver Hotel and bar.* I would come to spend
many an evening there drinking draft beer and playing pool. It was hard to spend
money at the Beaver as the locals kept my glass full, with a nod and a smile.

A word about the locals: no one locked their doors to their houses or cars. The car
keys were always in the ignition (probably the lowest rate of lost keys in the country);
you couldn't walk down a stretch of road without someone pulling over to ask you if
you needed a ride. Everyone waved at everyone else. It was scary. Where I came from,
if a stranger waved or smiled at you, you best start running in the opposite direction.
Maybe it was something in the water but Willet folks and surrounding towns were as
happy and friendly folk as I've ever met.

The directions I had were very good and I finally made it there. When I arrived that
first evening I drove up to the house. Of course, I didn't know a soul there and no one

had a clue of who I was. I immediately introduced myself as a friend of Oakes Plimpton and Paul Karapetian. Those were the magic words because I was immediately accepted as "one of the gang". Jarlath Hamrock was there and his acceptance was cautious but friendly. It wasn't many hours before I felt at home with a mix of personalities that were very interesting. Jarlath topped the list of interesting personalities when he declared that using the toilet in the house was disgusting and that everyone used the outhouse by the side of the house. No problem except the outhouse didn't have a door. If you wanted to use it, you had to start whistling loud enough for someone sitting on the throne to realize someone was coming so they could let out a loud and clear "occupied" before you could make the turn from the front of the house to the open view of the wooden structure with the occupant in some compromising pose.

I remember Irith, Jim Mihalyak, Lori, Mark and a few others whose faces I can see but whose names are long gone from my memory. I made one trip out there which lasted a month with Joe O'Rourke. Jarlath was the only other person there at that time. We (Joe and I) were going to make our fortunes as lumberjacks. We found work with a local contractor, no problem, but a dearth of pay. After working a month and getting one paycheck for about $200.00 for both of us with a promise of more to come, we set out to cash that baby. Everywhere we went all were willing to cash out the check even though we were strangers until they found out whose check it was. The dude we worked for had a reputation for miles around that was so bad — no one within fifty miles of his business would cash our check. We basically starved for a month and gave up dreams of being lumberjacks. After giving up in N. Y., Joe and I tried to get work in Jackman, ME, where we were turned down by the Scott Paper Co., so back we went back to Boston with great muscles and no money.

Back to Willet. I remember chopping wood (endlessly), milking the cow with one bad teat which Jarlath bought at auction. I was there for that event — no one wanted the cow with one bad teat so Jarlath picked it up for a good price. I remember chasing a pig on the loose and winding up with a permanently stained pig shit T shirt. It took six of us taking turns carrying it with its upturned feet to get it back into the pen. I remember skinny-dipping with four or five of the lovely young ladies down at the river at the bottom of the hill. You might say it was a thrill at the bottom of Mooney Hill. To get to the river, you had to cross a field looking in both directions for "the bull," all the while dodging cow pie mines everywhere. It was quite a feat to make it without hitting a pie. If you did step in one, well, there was always the river, but meeting the bull was never an option. I remember riding bareback on "Tarzan", Jarlath's horse. He stopped short from a gallop right in front of the house and sent me flying over his neck straight on to my ass. I was sore for a week. That was my first and last ride on the beast. I don't think he liked me because I would be talking to someone and he would come right up to me and bite me in the chest. He made like he was looking for sugar in my breast pocket, but I think he just liked biting me.

One day, Ray, Joe O'Rourke and I were driving down one of the country roads and a deer jumped in front of Ray's truck. We hit the deer, killed him dead instantly, threw him in the back of the pickup and drove back to the farmhouse. Mark, who liked to keep his hunting knife so sharp it could cleave a hole from this dimension into the next, strung the deer up in the barn and proceeded to gut the luckless deer. I was there with him and watched as he disemboweled that deer like a pro. As we were all starving, we had our fill once the deer cured a bit, hanging from a tree. I think it was November so it was cool enough not to rot. Jarlath ground the deer meat into hamburger, and I made a Sheppard pie or two over the next week. That deer did not go to waste, even the pigs got what was left over after the butchering. I remember cranking the milk separator so you could get milk out of one side and cream out of the other, it was a contraption, pure genius! I made butter out of the cream on one occasion, it was like magic to this city boy. Other adventures included "coon" hunting with O'Rourke (that's another whole story). There was another adventure when "Ace" (Craig Appel) came up. We decided to go hunting anything that moved, shotguns waving in the air and luckily missing everything we shot at. I was toting a 16 gauge single shot shotgun and was shooting at a group of pheasants from less than 50 feet away. They came away unscathed — oh happy day!

My favorite place in the house was the kitchen. We all took turns sitting around the old kitchen table just to talk about whatever came to mind. It was also a good place to be when supper was ready. The wood stove was something right out of grandma's childhood. It was fun stoking the stove, getting it ready to cook supper with the side benefit of adding heat to the kitchen. The living room was also a nice place to hang. I remember Oakes getting up on a big round coffee table and doing some kind of jig up there. I guess the spirit moved him. I have an old fuzzy photo of that event somewhere. I'd love to spend a week back there again when the place was in full swing.

To finish up, I remember walking out the front door of the farmhouse and seeing a hundred acres out in front of me (past the chicken coop) which led down to a grove of pines. You could walk left out the door and up the hill towards Staley's farm and you could see rolling pasture and perhaps a big buck running along the tree line. Off to the right you could set your gaze afar and look across the valley to the hills beyond. You could spend a week or a month and only see who you wanted to see. Willet, no traffic lights, no false pretenses, just farmers, farmlands, cows, trucks and a handful of city kids marveling at how simple life could be.

Jim Grossi
Groveland, Mass.

Jim Grossi sawing firewood by the barn.

<u>Splitting Rails in Willet, New York, fall of 1973</u> by Paul Karapetian
E-mail message from Paul, October 13, 2008, in response to my asking him for his Willet story, I guess you could say written in the style of Robert Service as in the Cremation of Sam McGee!

Well...OK, I guess, Oake. But I kin hardly remember what got spoke word fer word. Some folks got a talent that-a way, but I don't an' I never did. So I rekkin what the old man at Staley's farm said t' us boys that day I kin only guess at, that's all. But I'll tell ya what, tho. I kin remembers the ways thangs looks to th' neked eye ---kinda like a pitcher-post-card. An' I kin remembers how sartin things felt t' th' touch ---you know Oak--- how yer hands feel when they's a-touchin' cold or hot, thangs roughed up or smooth like. Mebbe that'll be enough fer ya, 'cep with some words thowed betwixt 'em. Anyways, that's all I kin do so I guess it'll have to be.

Come t' think of it, I bet ol' Joe w'd remember what got spoke that day better'n me! Fact is, I'll bet Joe's dis-remember more'n I ever re-membered 'bout those days! Smart like a tack, that Joe. All'uss studyin' on somethin'. Book-learned, too! Wern't he a piece o work, that Joe? Knife-an-a-fork, Joe O'Rourke. Hah! That's what they used t' call him. 'Member. Oak? Joe would set on a log, open up a can o' beans, an' that'd be his supper. I remembers onst that Joe an' I had us a con-test testin' which man would eat his supper faster than t'other. Well, we sat ourselves down one day t' dinner an' I was tryin' t' be not noticin' that we wuz con-testin' so I wuzn't even lookin', an' that's when I took mah first bite, then 'nother, an' I figger that's doin' purty good. Well, I'm takin' my last bite an' lookin up at Joe, and guess what, Oake? Joe's already sat back in his chair with his hands behind his hed an' grinnin' like a cat. Knife-an'-a-fork. Joe O'Rourke.

Oh, anyways. I remembers sleepin' in th' hayloft up th' Willet barn back then. Me an' Joe, we were kinda neighbors cuz he'd already been set up in th' hay-bales an' then I joined him one day, 'cep'n I wuz set up in the loft. Well, anyways, Joe wuz first a little angrified cuz he all'uss had th' barn to his own, but then he got used t' the idea that we wuz neighbors, an' then that wuz that.

Well, one day Joe says t' me that he got wind that neighbor Carl Staley had some work fer a couple o' fellers if they'd be willin' to sweat a bit. Me an' Joe figgered we wuz as good as th' next so we signed up that very day. We wuz t' be thar brite n' early next mornin', ready fer work. So we wuz. Brite an' early, we wuz at Staley's farm.

Ever split rails, Oake? It's farm work, all right. Take a bunch a big ol' logs jest layin' there waitin' t' get split so a fence kin git made or mended. Logs gotta get cut down t' size, then ya' set a steel wedge at one end what gits layed-to with a heavy maul. Split th' log that-a way, move th' wedge along in th' split an' lay-to with the maul onest more. Then agin an' agin 'till the log's split half-ways. Then those half-splits git split agin so's then ya gots a nice pile o' rails fer a proper fence! Carl Staley showed us boys how t' set a wedge in the grain so when the maul hits it true, th' log'll split clean. Carl knew wood all right.

Now, good hands on a farm kin split rails all mornin' then go out a'ter breakfast an lay the fence. Anyway, farmer Staley said so, so Joe an' I figgers we can, too, so we commenced to lay into that pile o' logs right away. Joe turnin' logs over one by one. Me settin' wedges an' tunkin' 'em in with a sledge. Then both of us takin' full swings with th' maul to split 'em up. Wern't long 'till me and Joe wuz a-sweatin jest like Carl Staley said we would. I remembers us takin' our shirts off cuz they got so wet so quik. We rolled them logs, an' set an' tunked them wedges fer a good hour. We got so fierce with them logs we din't notice Staley backin' off our business. I din't see him 'til I looked up an' he wuz walkin' away, shakin' his head a little and grinnin'. I remembers that grin wuz kinda like Joe's big ol' grin at our dinner eatin' contest, 'cep'n I wern't aware what Carl wuz grinnin' about. I also wern't aware o' how mah hands wuz beat up on th' wedges and scraped on the logs. But worst wuz how mah hands wuz gonna be on the wood-handle mauls. Carl knew, though. Mebbe that's what he wuz grinnin about. Soft hands on them rough hick'ry handles. Anyways, I din't look up at Joe an' he wern't lookin' at me. We wuz jist workin as hard as we could for as long as we could 'till we both saw an an old man git up from his chair at the other end of the yard an' walk our way.

"You boys are workin' that pile purty hard", the old man said, gittin up close. "No sense workin' so hard. There'll be more work when yer dead."

Me an' Joe jest looked at 'em, kinda sideways. Joe had a chaw workin' an' he spit some down an' he smiled an' said t' the old man, "What? What d'you mean? We ain't dead!" Joe leaned back his head and laughed. Joe had a kind of laugh where he'd laugh then he'd grin an' looked straight atcha t' see whether you be laughin' too. I kin see him there right now ---standin' a-top that pile o' split logs, leanin' his weight on his long-handle maul, terbacco juice dribblin down his chin, grinnin' as wide a grin as I'd ever seen him grin. Him grinnin' at me, then lookin' at the old man, then back at me...jist t' see who was laughin' with him. "Hey! We ain't dead...YET!", Joe laughed agin.

The old man turned to walk back to his sittin' place, but then he stopped. "You boys better go git somethin t' eat." he said over-shoulder, walkin' away. "Git up t' the house. Miz Staley's got brekfest ready."

Now I'd had me some piles o' food in my time, I guess. But me and Joe, we'd never seen nothin' like the table Miz Staley had ev'ry brekfest fer th' farmhands. They wuz bowls full of aigs n' taters, slabs o' ham, flapper-jacks, an' hot biscuits slathered in butter n' gravy. And th' milk! Whooee! Ever had cold fresh milk, Oak? It's like butter-cream, Oak. Like butter-cream.

Anyways, Miz Staley made sure her men got fed, but she could shoo them out the kitchen as fast as she reeled 'em in. "Now git!", she'd say an' all those men'd scrabble like little boys. Hah! Oh, I'll all'uss remembers Miz Staley an' that food, all right. An' Joe will too! I seed some o' them big broad men at that table jest starin' at Joe whilst he et pile on plate o' viddles. Mercy. That Joe could pack it in.

We spent that a'ternoon out in the fields, settin' posts an runin' wire. Went home tired, too. Came back th' next day, me with gloves on mah hands cause they wuz so blistered up from workin' at the maul's hick'ry handle. Joe wuz OK, tho, on account o' he wuz all'uss more a workin' man than me an' so his hands wuz callouse long a'fore we split our first log. Anyways, Carl laughed a little when he saw mah gloves, but that wuz all he did. Oh I guess he might-a taken his hat off and scratched his hed and laughed a little more, but that's all. Carl Staley wern't a man to make fun o' his men. He treated me an' Joe like we wuz family, really, an' th' same with everone else. Staley wuz a good man.

Well, anyway Oak, that's how me an' Joe larned t' mend fences whilst we wuz at Willet. But truth told, mostly I remembers how them maul-handles put a hurt on m' hands. That's what I remembers 'bout the work.

One more thang, tho...mebbe more like a dream or a 'memb'rence of a movin' pitcher. Anyways, I remembers the green, Oake. Everwhar green at Staley's farm. Green at the tree line. Rows o' green like store bought carpet on the back acres. Tall green grass, wavin' o'er Carl Staley's fields. He'd tow us out t' the fence-line in a horse-cart, me an' Joe sittin' on a short pile o' rails an' posts, bumpin' along on that rutty road. An' Carl's purty collie dog would be runnin' 'long side, th' dog's long blondy hair wavin' like the grass, an' that collie dog barkin' at Joe cuz he could smell Joe's hounds on 'em. I'm sure of that. An' when th' sun wuz settin' an' th' work done, he'd tow us back to the farmyard whar th' farmhands done brought up a fresh pile o' logs while we wuz out mendin' ---jest like th' pile that me an' Joe split 'fore brekfist. Mebbe bigger. Anyways, me an' Joe w'd climb out th' cart an' load into Joe's truck fer th' trip home. We'd wave t' Carl as we lit out th' yard. An' we'd wave at the old man, too, sittin' on his chair by th' new pile o' logs, him grinnin' at me, then grinnin' at Joe, then back at me.

Notes: Paul is an artist too, and follows two of his pen and ink drawings, one of a sunflower, two of Willet fences, presumably not ones that he and Joe made!

Sunflowers with seeds, P.K. drawing

Two drawings of fences at Willet by P. K.

Willet, 1974 to 2010

During the next year or two Jarlath bought the other partners out (principally George and Ira, George buying out David Beach first), to become its sole owner. As of October 2010 Jarlath still owns the farm at Mooney Hill Road, Willet, N. Y., renting out the fields to neighboring farmers, and living there when he's not at another farm near Ithaca or caddying on the professional woman's golf tour. He rents out the fields to neighboring farmers for hay and field corn. He still tends the grounds, and improved the land by putting in two farm ponds. In the late 1970s Jarlath became interested in the American Agriculture Movement — tractor-cades in protest of farm prices driven to D.C., and in attempting to write articles about the movement he was appointed the New York A.A.M. representative! Hence Willet became the N.Y. A.A.M. HQ! Jarlath could write another book about those years, but for the present I have collected his summary descriptions after the responses from the other farm participants. Then the 2008 farm reunion over Labor Day, 2008, is described.

Journal Responses — Life Before and After Willet

I invited the farm principals to write their response to this Journal, to give their perceptions of that 1972 season — how their circumstances led to Willet, what Willet meant to them, and then their subsequent lives in brief. Here's what I wrote everyone regards the Journal itself:

This Journal I have to say is a bit much, and I hope all of you won't get mad over my interpretation of events -- well, you can write your version!

Follows the 'life' stories and commentary of the farm founders and participants.

Founders Stories
—George Jacobs, Ira Karasick, Jim Ord, also Jill Jacobs

George Jacobs' Story

George contributed the following about his Willet experiences, but from hearing his tales at the reunion, and knowing he spent two winters and three summers there, we could have another book to present! Presently he's retired, married to Alexa, has two grown-up children, and works occasionally as a spiritual counseler when he's not gardening or playing music. He now lives in Gardener, N.Y. Here's his story:

I was born in Penciltucky (Pennsylvania), an only child of small town well-intentioned WASP parents. My father sold Hardwick ranges, my mom took care of the house, which was in the Back Mountain area, which means something if you live around Wilkes-Barre out toward Harvey's Lake. My spiritual father was the Holy Yost, that is, the Reverend Yost, also known as the "Skinner" for his many references to and interest in the skin of young people. The Skinner had taken me under his wing when I was part of a gang called the No-Tites (no titles, that is). I ultimately straightened out and was selected as a Rotary Exchange Student. I spent a year in the Philippines working with the Philippine Rural Reconstruction Movement, founded by one of those universal good guys named Jimmy Yen. I returned with sacks of winnowing and fish traps which I continued for a time to import and sell, sending the money back to the villages where they were made—doing my part to save the world.

Both before and after the Philippine experience, my escape from that brand of suffocating conditioning was toward the land and the unpretentious folk who were still attached to it. I found great release in plowing the earth and eventually growing many acres of sweet corn, tomatoes and melons along the Susquehanna and marketing them at my roadside stand. I was eventually joined in this by several kindred spirits, two of whom—Ira Karasick and Dick Bogdan—would later be part of the Willet farm. The Penciltucky State Police eventually drove us and my crew off that Susquehanna farm

83

I was renting from our good friend George Zarychta. The "eviction" shortly followed our attack on the 109th Field Artillery encamped on maneuvers on the neighboring farm. We interrupted their convoy by setting up a roadblock and throwing ears of corn as mock grenades—they responded appropriately, deploying in riot formation. After they set up tents, we drove through their camp with Frank Minelli's vintage Dodge, waving my grandfather's shotgun and exploding the silver salutes (M-80's) we used to scare blackbirds from the corn. We had some riotous fun for sure, but "the Staties" took it far too seriously, particularly a real asshole named Corporal Corbett, whose last words in court were "I'll get you, I'll get you." Appearing in front of the local magistrate, we defended ourselves and won our case, thanks largely to the appearance of Colonel Shimola of the 109th who said it was the most fun they'd had in a long time. But the police threatened George Zarychta with the loss of his farm through a legal suit brought by his estranged wife. With reluctance, he was forced to ask us to leave.

My pattern during those years was to work hard during the farming season and then leave the country, Jack Kerouac style, for high adventure in exotic places. On those vagabond excursions I lived the old adage, "Home is where the heart is" (I remember my mother saying this), and I added, "and when your heart is open, you are at home wherever you are."

Conditioned as a liberally educated Westerner, it was incumbent upon me to go to Europe, so on one of those winters I scoured New York for the cheapest way across the Atlantic. That turned out to be a Yugoslav freighter. Feeling both the terror and excitement of the unknown, I boarded her for the crossing. A day out of Tangier, the first port of call, I was captivated by the Arabic music coming over the radio and decided to disembark there for a few days. The few days became several months as I set up camp on the beach at Agadir in southern Morocco and was gifted Arabic lessons from a very special Moroccan woman named Khadija whom I have never seen again. There were surfers from Australia, Canada and the Isle of Jersey, all happily stoned by the sun, the sand, the magnificent surf and of course the ubiquitous hashish. Body surfing was spectacular. The waves were quite large and broke out far so that you had to get out over your head and tread water, waiting to catch one. When you did, you flew on its crest for a few breathtaking seconds before it churned you up and spit you out into the shallows. Just a few of those a day left me ecstatically quenched. Southern Morocco was paradise and it cost almost nothing. For a dollar you could fill a basket with oranges, pomegranates, vegetables, fresh baked bread, hummos, baba, fruits, olives of every description, all from the Agadir souk.

What finally prompted me to leave paradise was a postcard from Ira informing me that Marshall had bought a farm in Massachusetts and the people there wanted to farm it, but no one had farming experience. Would I come and help? I very quickly made plans to return to America, traveling up through Europe to pick up a cheap Icelandic flight to New York. So I did finally get to Europe, but it seemed mild and tame after my life in Morocco. After having struggled to learn enough Arabic to negotiate the Souk (an Arabian market), Spanish and French seemed pretty much like English and, by contrast, it felt comparatively easy to speak and understood both as I hitchhiked through those countries. I especially enjoyed sparring with the good-humored insults of the French. They were endearingly kind to me, picking me up off the road, taking me to their homes and feeding me so well.

The farm that Ira spoke of, in Montague, Mass., was found and secured by Marshall Bloom, the leader of a breakaway faction of the Liberation News Service in NYC, an intrepid source of news material for the underground newspapers proliferating at that time. As soon as I arrived there, I was challenged by the then radical ideas of organic farming and annoyed at the ideological self-righteousness of some of the group. I had received my foundational lessons in farming from Cy, our County Farm Agent, who was schooled in the "green revolution" of chemical agriculture. The term "organic" was not part of his or my vocabulary. I did pick up some of the traditional ways from Corey Crispell, Mike Silic and George Zarychta, and we did use manure, cover crops, in field composting and other more natural methods when we could, but we trusted in those 80 pound bags of 10-10-10. The more complex chemicals such as 2,4-D (a broadleaf weed-killer I later learned to be an ingredient of agent orange) and atrazine (the standard go-to weed killer for corn farmers) did not become available until a few years later. Innocent that I was, I accepted the prevailing methodologies and used the products. My skepticism began when a planting of corn susceptible to 2,4-D (a variety named Sugar King) literally "freaked out". Huskless ears grew out the top of the plant where the tassels should have been and contorted tassels grew in the ear's proper place. In the human species, this would be akin to penises growing on women and vaginas on men. So while I chafed at these inexperienced "radicals", these non-farmers who were telling me how to farm, I also listened and read and researched everything I could find on organic farming (at that time mostly a collection of Rodale's Organic Gardening magazines).

I was persuaded by the organic arguments and ready to take on the organic way, but still felt like an interloper at the farm. I had no ownership and the politics made it hard to make anything happen.

That winter I headed off for a tax-free teaching job in Saudi Arabia in order to accumulate enough cash to buy some land where we might be free to farm and live as we wanted. I returned from Arabia in 1970 with about 12,000 dollars, a lot of money for a young guy at that time. I bought a brand new Datsun pickup with a four cylinder OHC engine and five- speed transmission for $2000 and drove off in the direction of my farm friends in Massachusetts. It was a catalytic moment when I turned the corner at Pleasant Street, Amherst and Route 9 and there were Ira Karasick and Jim Ord looking for a ride.

Ira relates: "Actually, Jim and I were hitchhiking to Mexico. After George picked us up, we drove straight down to Miami Airport (I think we stopped in Boca Raton to see Chuck Malkemes, an old friend of George who was an engineer with IBM and whose sweet wife was terrified that George would lure Chuck away from swimming pool suburbia to some wild adventure). At Miami Airport we walked around the ticket counters, looking for a cheap flight anywhere that was leaving soon. We settled on the Cayman Islands, which none of us had heard of, and off we went. After that it gets blurry, except that Jim and George and I spent a week or two in the Caymans. Then I went north, and they went I don't remember where. They must have spent some time thinking about buying a farm and doing it their way, because when Jim and George came back, they headed right off to find a place."

It wasn't long before me and my buddies took what was left of that $12,000 and put a big down payment on a 350 acre farm! Franz Leenders, a friend from Holland and I, were the first to show up on that hilltop in Willet, NY, Spring of '71. Our first project was to build a solar shower using the top of the old well house to support the collector. The daughter and son-in-law of Grandma Pearl Crittenden, the lady who sold us the farm, showed up with a case of beer and we resurrected the chicken coop. Jim Ord made the trip from Massachusetts with a 10- ton dump truck he had personally reconditioned. Ira recalls, "I think Jim bought that truck from a Polish onion or potato farmer/contractor in North Hadley, Mass. It had five forward gears and a two speed axle with an electric button switch on the gear stick. It had air brakes which had be adjusted now and then or they would simply fail, particularly with a heavy load on a steep hill." That dump truck was destined to haul countless loads of chicken manure from a nearby farm and lime from a Syracuse quarry. In the back of the dump was a 1939 hand crank John Deere A tractor that plowed the fields, loaded the manure, and ran the ensilage chopper and cordwood saw. The elemental ingredients—manure, lime, wood, sweat and beer.

My best friend Ira caught up with us — we had farmed together in Penciltucky—and oversaw matters of legality and finance, as best one could in such a milieu. Dick and Caesar showed up from Delaware Valley Ag School (Dick had been head corn picker in Penciltucky). Those first years were ones of high spirits and hard work. There are so many tales to tell: Ivy the Pig, Scrotum the Dog, my cousin Jill and her dog Borschk, Hamish McLean of Scotland, Mihaliyak, Oakes the Farmer/Benefactor, Popeye, Clem, Chica (Mary Beth Annarella), Linda Lamb from Kansas, Angelo, Chino and the young-bloods from lower Manhattan, Dick Mann (who eventually made off with the Datsun),

George Sherman, Michael Curry who made all new windows for the old farmhouse, Pete Winters, a local tractor mechanic who helped keep things running, Alan McKee who loaned us farm equipment, uncle Jack Bevan who installed electric service in the old farmhouse, Barbara Hughey, Irith Goldman, Claire Ahlquist, Kathy Karis, Dana Wilner, Mike Huston, Chad Higgs (who eventually married Grandma Pearl's granddaughter)— all these beings and more, some local and some from far away places, lived, worked or helped out on the Willet Farm during its first few years of high activity.

We had a love affair with that rural upstate Appalachia community. I mentioned that Chad Higgs, also from Penciltucky, (friend of Dick Bogdan's step brother Mike Huston) married Grandma Pearl's gorgeous granddaughter Donna. Jim had been dating her, but marriage was not on his agenda at the time, and he graciously consented to Chad's firmer plans. Clem Kastings of Willet was a ubiquitous figure on the hill, engineering and supervising the construction of a ceramic flue lined chimney that rose from the basement floor and ran through the center of the house, venting both the Home Comfort wood cook stove and the Round Oak Duplex parlor stove. These two great stoves fed us, warmed us and gave us life, especially through the intense winters.

When the weather got cold, most of the crew left for school, real jobs, the city— leaving a few of us to milk the cows, feed the pigs, split the firewood and keep things going. The farmhouse that came with the 350 rolling hilltop acres we bought was built in the mid 1800's, probably from the huge crop of trees on the property. By the time we arrived it was an Andrew Wyeth painting, a classic post and beam structure with sagging windows and skewed clapboards hanging like pieces of flesh from its skeleton of hand-hewn timbers. Here and there, where the missing clapboards lined up with the spaces between the wide plank hemlock sheathing, and through the holes in the hand-plastered walls, you could see clear through to the outside.

For some impractical reason, perhaps the view, the house was built on the west slope of the first rolling ridge, so that it caught the brunt of the strong northwesterlies. One very early winter morning, stumbling downstairs to stuff more cordwood into the Round Oak Duplex, I encountered a living-room snowdrift, a couple feet high and several feet long, reaching from a crack in the windward wall to within a few feet of the parlor fire.

Depending on the weather, and on one's mood and attitude, winter at Willet could be either exhilarating, deliciously challenging and astonishingly beautiful, or overwhelming, unendingly grey and inescapably depressing. When it was the latter, as it often was for me, the few of us crazy enough to remain on the farm through the winter would seek refuge in The Beaver, (the Brown Beaver Hotel), the alcoholic heart of Willet. I was one of those few, and one of the first to seek such refuge. Of course, as any inebriate will eventually confess, alcohol is no refuge. There is no balm in alcohol—only a short and costly escape from whatever form of suffering our karmic programming has arranged and our current life circumstances have triggered.

It was one of those times, one of those nights at The Beaver, my cousin Jill and I, looking for comfort at the breast of mother alcohol, I drank, without relief, to the point of seeing double. Further escape was needed. We decided to go to the only place we could think of that might feel most like home—Western Massachusetts and our farm friends—Dan, Nina, Betsy, Susan, Sam, Janice, George, Terry, Margaret, Stevie, Harvey, and more.

We took off, directly from The Beaver, in a 1960's junker, but in my state, I failed to negotiate the first turn in the road and drove directly into out neighbor's swamp. It must have been about 1 a.m. Drunk and frenzied, I commandeered the nearest farm truck and drove it into the swamp thinking that I could somehow use it to pull out the car. Now there were two swamped vehicles, our car and our neighbors' truck.

Jill, who was 16 at the time and at her height of cuteness, was often the apple of local male eyes. She flagged down the first car—it was the constable, an older kind gentleman, who was more than happy to take her to Popeye's. Popeye could get you out of any jam, not only because he had the necessary equipment, but because he'd been in so many himself. We had met Popeye months earlier in the Brown Beaver when, in the role of protective uncle, he had latched onto Jill. Popeye (Ed Zeeuw was his real name) called himself an old Dutchman, and with his pipe and twinkle, looked as close to the cartoon Popeye as I've ever seen. Soon Popeye, pipe dangling from the side of his mouth, showed up with tractor and tow chains, and within minutes we were back on the road.

Somewhere between Syracuse and Albany, we ran out of gas. Still quite drunk, I set off hitchhiking to the nearest gas station. This time it was the State Police that came by. Somehow I was able to disguise my drunkenness and the two gentlemen escorted me to a gas station, returned me to our car with gas and wished us a pleasant trip. The sun was coming up as we crossed the mountains into Massachusetts.

Messages from Jill Jacobs, George's Niece and Farm Partner

*Jill now works as an educational administrator in
Stanford, Conn., and is a single mother of Zhen, aged 16.*

Oakes, please try to remember, as I will, that I was a <u>teenager.</u> Believe me, I also cringe at a couple of vivid memories I have of my *antics,* so to speak. I was a wanna' be "hood"— never quite made it into that circle. It's sort of similar to New Canaan kids as wanna' be rappers.

Oakes, I was not very nice to you. (hindsight being 20/20) I don't even really understand why I was so rude to you. It must have been part of my *being cool, being "functionally" independent,* mode. I'm thankful you'll even talk to me now; although, it is probably much larger in my mind than yours.

Thanks, Jill

Oakes, THANK YOU for all of this. I so loved the veggie stand. I met this beautiful soul who gave me a job and fed me grilled cheese when times were rough while I was working at that stand. We wore George's clothes imported from Saudi Arabia.

Jill

WILLET PRODUCE? — <u>Account by Ira Karasick, Founder and Partner</u>

It was always a thought whether to write it with a question mark. Willet began with Jim Ord, George Jacobs, Jim Lesser (Caeser), Dick Bogdan and I, though of course each of us had a history. I didn't know it then, but later, when the movie *Deer Slayer* came out (1978), I knew that my four partners, all from Pennsylvania, were characters in that movie — Pennsylvania mill towns – Palmerston, Wilkes-Barre, Back Mountain. . . But we bought Willet in 1971 from Pearl (Crittenden) Doty. I can't remember if it was her brother or husband that farmed it—or part of it; the farm was really two hill farms put together to make up about 350 acres. But I remember his name – Julius Caeser Ebenezer Crittenden, who was called "'Nezer" for short.

The town of Willet had about as many people as we had acres – 350. There were many more cows than people, and many many more deer than cows and people combined. You would have thought that the deer were reindeer, since you saw herds of them; I am not sure I ever saw regular old deer herd anywhere else. Willet was poor, Appalachian poor, which is what the Southern Tier of New York State was about, Appalachia, that is, and deer were shot and eaten year round, without regard for the hunting season. The deer when consumed this way were commonly called "government beef."

People in Willet had real character, that is, that they didn't find the need to obey the law and they hated (or at the very least strongly distrusted) any government outside the town. State police were not welcome. Especially when they came to bust one of the town's favorite and most exciting activities – cock fighting.

Pearl lived in a trailer. I met her on a cold April day. There is a picture that C. E. Green took of George and Jim Ord and I, leaning against the vomit green Datsun pickup George bought when he got back from Saudi Arabia, in the mud at the end of Wendell driveway, with my 48 Dodge power wagon behind, on the day that we

89

drove out to meet Pearl (I think they already had) and make the deal to buy Willet. I remember how beautiful it was up on the hill – beautiful and cold and windy. I remember my words – it's freezing, it's beautiful, buy it and let's get out of here.

Everything about Willet was intense, even when nothing was apparently going on.

Stories: Dan, me, Tom Fels? Yago? To Willet – stopped by the cops in upstate NY; cops thought Dan might be Karl Armstrong, the bomber of the Univ of Wisconsin math building (after Kent State), who was a fugitive at the time. Dan had no i.d. at all except he finally found a receipt in his pocket for getting his cow Daisy fucked — that is, inseminated, and who could make that one up?

Dick Bogdan was the head picker (corn picker, that is) at the Keelersburg Hotel. The Hotel was an old 18th/19th century ordinary roadhouse along the Susquehanna River near Tunkhannock PA in the long since defunct town of Keelersburg. Here George, rather than get a summer job during college, rented a farm from George Zarychta (the "Mayor") in the summer of 1968, grew 20 acres of sweet corn (Silver Queen and Seneca Chief), 4 acres of tomatoes (that 4,000 plants per acre) and one acre of melons on black plastic. George collected a mixed (up) crew including me and Dick Bogdan, who had an older sister Susie that George fooled around with, and many others, who are a whole other story. We had three farm stands where we sold the produce; we bought bags of morning glory seeds but we grew no morning glories; and had numerous adventures as the sole outpost of hippiedom in greater Wilkes Barre among the Am Legion and VFWs. Caeser I didn't know before; he was Dick's friend. I don't think I ever got to know him. Dick, I think, went off with Linda Lamb (what a great name), a girl who had answered an ad we placed at Wendell for girls to live on that farm. She arrived at Wendell driven by her father— she had come from Kansas or Nebraska and graduated from Stanford—and Frans had entertained her, but the women at Wendell —Clare Margaret and Betsy, were hard on her and when we bought Willet she came right out there with George and I. I have no idea what has become of her.

It was at Keelersburg that I got the bug for farming. After the season George and I built a house on the back of a flatbed International truck, complete with two beds, a rocking chair, a wood stove and a picture of Emiliano Zapata hanging on the wall, and set off for points north. We headed for Montague Mass because we had read of the founding of the Liberation News Service farm, and Marshall Bloom, who George knew from Amherst. We arrived there on a beautiful fall day. I and the truck ended up staying the winter; George headed off for Morocco. But that was how we hooked up with the "farm crowd."

Every once and a while the people who came through pop into my head. Vesla, a dark haired dark eyed woman from a commune called Owl Creek, that I think broke up, came with her baby and stayed for a time. It could have been a week or a month. I remember the day Mary Beth (Chica) Anarella arrived. The first time that I saw her she was riding behind George on one of the tractors — she was olive oil, dark and small and intense. She came from around Pittsburgh, somehow finding Willet among all the communal gin joints up and down the East Coast.

Hamish was sent to us by Bob Rodale. Hamish came from Scotland. He was visiting organic farms and communes around the U.S. to prepare for one day taking over his family estate and creating an organic community there. He lived in Breda House, Alford, Aberdeenshire, where he had the whole nine yards — thousands of acres and the manor house and moor and collies. His mother had been at a séance in England, London, I think, and had learned that Hamish was destined to lead a natural community.

Frans Leenders was born in Indonesia, and grew up in Den Helder, in Holland, he was going to medical school and had taken his wanderjahre in the States. He had traveled over the Atlantic the first time with Hans; they met a girl named Barbara Kleckner, who gave them her friend Terry Rodgers address in Wendell. Hans and Frans agreed to meet at the Wendell farm, though neither had been there or knew anyone there (except Terry's name). I was living at Wendell then, and I was working on the shop, a barn-like building where Dan and Nina now live. Hans comes walking down the road – you need to know that the road is a dead end off a tee on the side of a hill with no other houses but ours. So people didn't just walk up the road. I'm Hans, he says. I'm here to meet Frans. And who is Frans? Well, an hour or so later, Frans comes walking up the road.

Now Frans was back again, this time with Julie Katan. Later they would marry and have two daughters, Rosa and Eva, and a son, Frans. But now they were kids, though Dutch people seemed older than the rest of us. Frans has an easy birthday to remember, August 6, 1945.

Jerry, sitting in his white pickup truck at the crossroads with his shotgun, waiting . —for me?[*] He was pure paranoia—if you could bottle paranoia, that was Jerry. Living in McDonough, another lost town in the Southern Tier, in a very fixed up farmhouse with Alexa, glaring and showing off and disappearing regularly to nowhere New York City. By the end of the long Willet winter, the second one, I think, because the summers and winters really do combine and the years are indistinct, Jill ended up with

---

[*]   Jerry subsequently wrote me that he was waiting for that someone who was stealing his firewood — he suffered some bad relations with the locals. In general we were very appreciative of his support of our farming venture -- several times he rescued us with machinery he had access to. And we had the luxury of visiting his civilized house — the Willet farmhouse was very rough.

Jerry and George with Alexa. I am sure it worked out better for George than for Jill, although Jill had a interesting run.

I remember events — trading a load of sawdust for a huge pail of cultivated blueberries, which we picked on the side of a hill and making blueberry wine (that was Jim Ord's passion); Jim's baler all tangled up with buckwheat — little tetrahedrons, I think the grain was, and taking bags of buckwheat up to a stone mill on Lake Cayuga to grind into dark flour. I don't remember conversations, like in Oakes' journal. Yet when I read about them, the words come back to me, sometimes amazed that I could have been so narrow and pigheaded.

IRA—POST WILLET

You remember it was Ira that pulled out his calculator to figure out that Willet Produce as a farm was untenable financially. I just talked to him by phone last night, July 15, 2010. Now he is a lawyer living in Montclaire, New Jersey, with a practice in litigation and land use (zoning, planning), his family at his in-laws place in Marthas Vineyard while he is holding down the fort in N. J. recuperating from an operation on his shoulder. And more recently still, as this book is going to press, Ira sent me some more Willet photos, one of the signing of the papers to buy the farm!

After Willet Ira had to make up credits in order to graduate from Amherst, so he took some courses at Hunter College in New York and graduated, and then applied to graduate school. Law school. He got a really high score in the SAT's, but his Amherst grades were not good. He applied to a number of law schools, but was turned down by all of them save Brooklyn and Harvard! He only applied to Harvard because an Amherst teacher, Conrad Kent, refused to give him a recommendation unless he applied there! Then he called me, and it turned out I had an apartment free for him to live in in Cambridge.

Ira did very well at Harvard, Magna Cum Laude, and became a friend and acolyte of Professor Lawrence Tribe. I remember Ira making bookcases for him. Working with Tribe got him some interesting assignments such as drafting a constitution for one of the Micronesian islands. After law school Ira became a member of the Anti-Nuclear coalition, organizing the great fund-raising concert to raise funds and consciousness versus the Seabrook Nuclear power plant. Aside from his New Jersey law practice, Ira has dipped into politics, and back in 1993 he ran for the mayor of Hoboken (unsuccessfully).

Ceasar, Ira and George at the Willet closing.

Oakes, George and Ira on the tractor.

Account by Jim Ord, Founder — Prequel

Of all the communes and people that I came into contact with during that golden back to the land period of the late sixties and early seventies, my situation is somewhat unique. I came from a background that was closely involved with farming and mechanical skills. Although my parents were educated professionals, they chose to live in the countryside largely populated by the industrious Pennsylvania Dutch farmers. My childhood thus was split between influence from a Yale educated Connecticut Yankee and Sonny, a dear soul of amazing strength and a disposition emanating from his moniker. From the time I was six years old until I'd finished high school, whenever there was work to be done in the fields I was there, first just riding along on the fender of the old Fordson and later helping however I could. From picking rocks to bailing hay, from bagging grain on the combine to spring plowing.

From that background came a natural aptitude for accomplishing work and for fixing things. To illustrate the extent to which I was exposed to the self reliant life style, at the age of 14 Sonny had me clipping, rasping, and shaping my horses hooves, then resetting the shoes being careful not nail into the quick. Who does that? Ask any horse person here in 2010 if they would even think of doing that for themselves.

With all that in mind it should not surprise anyone that I dropped out of college in 1968, bored with the pursuit of some intangible future as a cog in what I thought of at that time as the machine. My dreams were to live closely with the land. To be connected to the source of my existence. To make for myself that which I needed to sustain me. Toil was not something to be reviled but rather to be celebrated as part of the balance — to not only understand, but to feel the justification of your existence. Hence for me, the back to the land movement of the hippies was like a siren call. Not to lessen the influence of the antiwar, brotherhood of man, free love, we can change the world dawning of the Aquarius thing.

I was ripe. Having attended college in western Massachusetts probably set the stage for all that followed. That part of the world is, if not unique, certainly remarkable in the manner of attracting thinking people and accepting diversity. With its plethora of colleges and beautiful countryside, it's no wonder that so many communes and other alternate lifestyles of the rural kind have rooted there.

How Willet Produce came about from my perspective

After dropping out of college, I moved to North Leverett, to live with a friend and former teacher at Springfield College. Trenor shared, if not my enthusiasm for farming, an excitement for the times. He and his wife Roberta had a small fallow farm at the base of Mt Toby which they allowed me to use and live on. I quickly got to work signing a contract with Oxford Pickle Co to raise five acres of cucumbers. The fact that all my previous experience had nothing to do with produce of course meant nothing. I was off and running. I sold my Yamaha to buy a John Deere. I fixed up a derelict old plow and harrow enough to use and ran full steam ahead. No barrier could stop me, I was changing the landscape, and I was setting the world on fire. Then the rains came during blossom, a two week period during which pollination occurs so baby cucumbers can form. Guess what? Bees don't work in the rain. Not much of a crop.

During that year, however, I met people who would change the path if not the course of my life. There was Marshall and all of the folks at the Montague farm. Stemming from that association was a meeting with two other people key to the chronology of the journey to Willet. George Jacobs, a most charismatic world traveler and former corn grower in PA passed through to visit old Amherst friends before shipping out to teach English in Saudi Arabia. George visited me at my cucumber venture and we became quick friends sharing many common interests. The other person was Dan Keller currently finishing his film studies at Amherst and a frequent visitor at the Montague farm.

With fall of that year I left Trenor and Roberta to spend the winter in PA working at a factory to pay off debts and in spring accepted an invitation to join Dan and friends on a venture of back to the land communal living. As anyone who was part of that movement at that time can attest, life moved at warp speed. Lifelong friendships were forged, buildings were built, land was tilled, engines were rebuilt, animals were raised then slaughtered, and still there was music made and life celebrated. There were sibling farms, i.e: Packers Corner, Montague, Wendell, and cousin farms as well such as the Johnson Pasture. Some key players in all this were individuals such as Jim Aaron and Steve Sayre and Fred Hayes and Mark Kramer. The hills were alive with energy and social experiment as we youth were trying to make life evolve differently than we witnessed in the good old USA.

According to the Willet Founding Father Match Book series, there were three of us, Jim Ord author of this part of the narrative, George Jacobs aforementioned, and Ira Karasick. Ira, once described as a "whip smart Jewish Kid from Long Island", met George at Amherst and spent a summer working and playing on Georges PA summer sweet corn venture. He also dropped out of college to live at Montague where Ira and I became fast friends and were at times referred to as the kids (we were 2 or 3 yrs younger than most) and often ran off together on ventures and adventures. Ira later moved to Wendell where I was living that following summer.

Wendell farm was idyllic, but nothing is perfect and there was a bit of disagreement on the importance of work vs. the importance of lifestyle, hence the tensions developing between the artists and the workers. It is important to me to remember that although this tension existed and at times approached strife, the caring and respect we had for each other was resilient and I still feel a kinship to all who were part of that experience. The tension is important to the Willet saga because it allowed for the desire to create more of a "working farm" oriented commune.

That December, on the spur of the moment, Ira and I decided to hitch hike to Guatemala. Journeys like that were a rite of passage for us. Ira had done, I was a virgin. At this point the story becomes unbelievable but true. We were standing Rt. 9 and Rt. 63 in downtown Amherst in the snow with our thumbs out when a Datsun pickup pulled to the curb. Yea, a ride. Ira opened the passenger door and the next thing I knew, dove in headlong. I peered in to find him hugging George. Unbelievable. George asked "where ya headed?" Ira answered Guatemala. George answered get in, me to. George had been working and saving in Saudi for almost 18 months, but needed to be out of the US for an additional 6 weeks to qualify for tax breaks.

For the next three months a travel adventure that never reached Guatemala but did see Grand Cayman, Mexico from top to bottom, and the width and breadth of the good old USA from Mt St Helens to the Florida Keys. 10,000 miles of thumbing and a story for another time. During that trip a decision to return and buy a farm to really get into serious organic farming was made.

THE ROAD TO WILLET

We returned end of March to Wendell, announced our plan, squeezed (I am six feet tall, George must be six two, and Ira is wider than both of us) into the cab of Georges Datsun and headed off farm shopping with the United Farm Realty catalogue as our road map. It is important to remember how compressed everything was in those days. I quit school in spring 1968 and here I was on this adventure in spring of 1971 with two farm experiences behind me, whew. We looked briefly in Massachusetts and eastern NY and although those areas held cultural appeal, land was far too valuable for us. In fact we frequently sang "It's a hard world to get a break in, all the good land has been taken." The lure of cheap farms took us north to the St Lawrence valley of NY. Bleak at that time of year. Stand on the roof of the truck to see over the snow banks to see the lay of the farms we were touring. Towns like Goveneur, Herman, others. Flat mostly, cheap sure, but not appealing.

We decided to head for PA for some home cooking, a day or two R&R, then off to Eastern Oregon where cheap farmland was advertised. As fate often intervenes, we were descending Rt. 81 toward PA and stopped in Cortland for gas right next to a United Farm Realty office. Without expectation we went in to inquire, fully expecting things this far south to be out of our price range. The realtor showed us a farm to the west that was nice but not right and then took us to Willet. As we drove to the top of that hill on a beautiful spring day early in April, with patches of snow still laying about where the wind had made it deep and the sun hadn't found it yet. We learned that there were 350 acres (half of a square mile) on the highest farm land in Courtland

County and we could have it for 37,000 dollars. I remember getting out of the car and walking to the top of the hill above the run down old house. The sun was warm, the sky was clear and I could see forever. I was smitten. This was it. George & Ira may not have felt as passionately as I, but certainly agreed that this was to be our farm. We bought it. My father asked "Willet Produce"?

POST WILLET

As already mentioned, Jim left Willet after the first year, disillusioned with the chaos and difficulties (lack of focus and direction) — of farming communally. He bought a trailer in Willet and lived there the year I lived there, and he would come to visit from time to time. The following is a summary transcription of a telephone interview I had with him July 5, 2010, 95 degrees out here in Arlington, and no doubt the same in Pennsylvania!

Jim told me that when he first bought his house in Palmerton, PA, a fixer upper, he thought that he would eventually make enough money to entertain the dream of buying a farm and farming. But no, that moment never came, he still lives there, and he made his career out of carpentry and home building, primarily log homes. He has a large garden, and couple of acres to maintain. He's married to Nancy from Jim Thorpe, Pennsylvania, and they raised four children, two boys and two girls, the oldest now 30, youngest 20. Two of his sons live in Alaska—Juneau, and are involved in construction and fishing. His two daughters are both good athletes, winning scholarships in softball and field hockey, and his older daughter is pursuing a career in physical education.

Presently Jim is working on resurrecting a 25 year abandoned log home he had originally built, and mostly works on home additions and alterations. He has talked of putting up a log cabin at Willet, but in the scheme of things, seems unlikely. He visited Willet a few weeks ago, calling up Jarlath to arrange. Here's what Jarlath wrote of his visit: *"Jim Ord stopped by Mooney Hill with his family (mother and son) last week. Great to see him. His mother looked in good health and is still attractive at 87! Son looked strong and alert."*

1972 Partner Stories
—Claire Ahlquist, Kathy Karis, Dana Wilner

Claire Ahlquist's Story

July 28, 2008

Hi Oakes,

Yes, I did get your snail mail, and was going to write back. And now your message via Brian and e-mail about the reunion. Unfortunately I have had a visit from my mom and sister on the calendar for Labor Day weekend for some time.

I will copy and send the few pictures I have from my Willet time with questions and comments.

<u>How I Got to Willet!</u>

I was living that summer (1971) at Wendell Depot in western Mass. — a rented farm-house with Meg and Carl Parsons, who invited me and others to live communally and grow a big garden. Also there was David Black, a writer, and his wife; another couple whose name I can't remember — a beautiful girl with curly red hair; also my friend Lynn, who came to visit Willet. Later Ron Newsome and Marianne Randjelovic arrived. This really was a wonderful time. I loved the gardening. We had a making dinner schedule, and we had great fun dinners every night. I did yoga in my room before dinner. I had a big brass bed that Jim Aaron, my man-friend at the time lent me, and helped me move over — boy was it heavy!

We had a preponderance of Taurus's including myself and Carl, and we joked about that in terms of Taurus supposed earthiness — the preponderance of scatological humor that spring up at our (stoned) dinner conversation. Also and best we had a swimming hole just a short jog through the woods where we skinny-dipped after getting all hot and sweaty and dirty in the garden.

It was so much fun at the end of the summer Meg and Carl decided to go get regular jobs and make enough money for a down payment on a farm somewhere, to start a communal organic farm. Well, at some point Ira told me about George Jacobs and him starting a new communal organic farm in Willet, New York, and invited me to come. At some point I decided to go!

WILLET

Journal comment: Re the journal, one area of personal sensitivity would be re my miscarriage. I arrived at Willet having unbeknownst to me conceived. Because I had had a Dalkon Shield IUD placed when I was in Massachusetts I never thought I could be pregnant and had ignored indicators. So I only found out I was pregnant when Jill and Dianne took me to the hospital in Cortland for the heavy bleeding I thought was a period, and found out I was miscarrying. The area of sensitivity is that your journal referred to it as an abortion the second time it was mentioned — could you please include a foot note in future copies. I don't believe I would have decided to terminate this pregnancy if I'd had a choice. I'm pro choice of course by the way. For the record I can't believe I'm so into this. Must be by way of greater understanding of my own past as well as that amazing time. — *I wrote back that I would certainly excise such reference — sorry for the lack of understanding.*

Kudos for presumably, apparently unselfedited transcription of your journal. Totally fascinating, and for me excruciatingly embarrassing re my comment during the potato seed cutting "scene." I've never had a good memory and have no remembrance of that scandalous bit of information or the reference for it — perhaps from one of the Marxist feminist writers I was wont to read at that time. These are things I am unlikely to come out with these days in casual conversation. But I can recall with fond nostalgia those days of unself-censuring freedom of expression. Speaking of censorship, please do share my communication online with the group, and the same would go for anyone else I've talked to online.

Other off the cuff reactions to your journal. Wow! Remember all that machinery breaking down and all that getting stuck! All that mud and chicken shit we shoveled and spread! I had little memory of our power struggles infighting not to mention actual fighting or philosophical and policy disagreements, but now can recall. The food sounds a lot better and more varied than I recalled. . . .

Hand-written pages: — At Willet I remember eating lots of scrambled eggs, rice, and zucchini as it was a rainy summer, and a lot of plants drowned. But the chickens were laying and the zucchini growing.

I remember enjoying harrowing the fields on the tractor (and almost tipping over once!). I <u>liked</u> driving that tractor. I remember the manure spreader getting stuck in the mud — again the rainy season. I remember weeding, and Oakes you weeding and driving the tractor.

I remember being scared to death by the ghost that walked across the tin roof of the barn where I had my sleeping nook over where Kathy's horse was stabled. I remember I was so scared I asked Ira and Kathy if I could sleep on the floor of their room after I moved from the barn to the house, for Jill had an encounter with the ghost coming into her room one night, and also making the piano stool swivel. I remember the ghost walking across the roof of the barn close to Jill's room in the house. It didn't bother me until I heard someone talking about "The Ghost" at the kitchen table — it was <u>the word</u>, <u>the idea</u> of ghost that scared me to death — was seriously freaked out!

We decided he was a previous owner, the guy who kept the exotic birds and fed the deer and other animals up on the hill. I remember the hills above the farm had a very 'spiritual' feel to them. Anyone with stories about the ghost, I'd love to exchange notes *(these memories written before reading the Journal).*

I remember going for ice cream (home-made) in the truck to the next town. I remember two guys that had come back from Afghanistan (buying and dealing drugs). I remember a guy named Hamish from Scotland. I remember I learned to weld (or tried to) working on putting together a vegetable stand on wheels we were trying to make out of a hay wagon. I remember rain, rain, rain! That's about it. . . .

Claire and her dog Burlap in the Barn 'Window'.

Claire's Journal

Turns out Claire kept a journal too! She found it and sent portions of it to me. It was more a diary of her inner process than a journal of farm life. I decided my journal is enough for this book! We will send hers to the Archives at the University of Massachusetts under the name *Total Loss Farm Archives, Willet Produce Farm, New York State*. My journal too. The archive was organized by Tom Fels, who wrote about the Amherst area communal farms under the title *Farm Friends*, RSI Press, 2008.

After Willet

After I left Willet, I went on my cross-country trip with my dog Burlap in my 1960 blue VW bug, with a tent and sleeping bag. I visited friends and saw some of the country — the Badlands, the Black Hills, Boulder, the Grand Tetons, the Rockies, Washington and Oregon, the Giant Sequoias, the California coast down to San Francisco and Haight-Ashbery, Reno, Salt Lake City. My favorites were the Badlands and the Black Hills of South Dakota, home of the Ogala Sioux, and my deepest experience at the Reservation of Wounded Knee.

So I had some adventures before settling down for some years at Birdsfoot Farm in Canton, New York. (I got a letter from Carl Parsons and Meg Spurlin at Willet inviting me there — that was the farm they had bought). We were a communal organic farm, and for some time I felt deeply and happy at home there. Until we pushed the envelop too far with experimentation, exploration of the limits of personal relationships. Unhappy, I left to try a new life. I did <u>love</u> the farming and the land, it was a painful thing to be separated from the place.

By and by I went to Nursing School (though I had graduated from college previously) to gain a skill to make a living at, and because of my interest in women's health issues, an out-growth of the women's movement I was involved with. This turned out to be a good move as becoming a nurse led to me becoming a women's Health Nurse Practitioner, a profession I have enjoyed very much as it has sustained me.

Brian and I married in 1979. We met protesting an electric power line they wanted to run through our area, with huge ugly towers, etc. (and they did). His daughter, my step-daughter, is now 30, and getting married next spring in Costa Rica, an event we very much look forward to. She has been a great pleasure as a child, a girl, and then a grown woman, a costume designer who lives in Santa Monica, California. Brian and I went on to have two sons, Adam, now 27, and Nicholas, 23, both struggling to find their paths. They too have given us much joy, as well as the usual problems youths and young men can face, and which parents must contend with. I find comfort in the memory of my own tumultuous years of confusion and anguish in my 20s. I trust they will find their way to contentment and satisfaction as I have.

Marrying Brian was my second good life decision — hard to believe it will be 30 years next year — best thing I ever did, though mostly it was good fortune, as it seemed to happen without a lot of thought. We're happy together and totally committed.

I don't think there's ever been a year I haven't put in a garden, even at the various places I rented. Oh yes, there was one — it was a bad time. But only one! The one I have this year is doing well. I've had rhubarb, peas, beans, zucchini, potatoes, spinach, greens, garlic, onions, tomatoes, peppers, and eggplant (maybe), and winter squash coming. In season I buy what I can at the farmers market. We also buy our beef, chicken, turkey locally, although I myself am a vegetarian and have been for many years.

Claire and her Mom — 2007 — 59 & 87

Kathy Karis

Kathy Karis now lives in Jupiter, Florida, works as a consultant, and has a large garden with a mulberry tree, and a papaya tree, also four horses and a goat!

Oakes,

What great memories you are giving us. No way I can make the reunion but I'll be there in spirit. And I will be in Boston on July 15- 20 next week just in case you are in town. Very best regards to all of you!

I have told that ghost story you mentioned *(Journal page 60)* so many times since then and people always are unsettled by it.

Here's a memory I have: me trying to make it through the winter with only myself and Dana and giving up the night before Thanksgiving. I rented a Uhaul horse trailer for my horse, dropped him off at the local riding stable, and made it to Boston for Thanksgiving dinner with my parents. It was so cold in Willet at that time that my fanny actually got frost bite while I was feeding the horse one morning. We couldn't get him loaded into the trailer for a long time, and the snow was falling. We walked over to the bar and asked if anyone could help us. A really fat man got a rope and his buddy and practically lifted Enterprise into the trailer.

Kathy

Dana Wilner

Dana Wilner lives in New York City near Greenwich Village with her partner David Palmer. She got a degree in graphic arts, and worked for the N.Y.C. Parks department for a number of years.

August, 2008

Hello Oakes,

I understand that you are trying to organize a "reunion" of Willet people? This is Dana Wilner replying via an email from Jim Ord. I hope this finds you well! Good to hear from some people from that time and place.

I told Jim that I am most likely going to England (Cornwall mostly) in the first week of September with my companion, David Palmer, and I am not sure I can organize myself enough to get to a gathering over Labor Day, but I hope you will send me details in any case, as I would be glad to know of what is happening and where. I would also be glad to at least have some email or mail correspondence regarding you, Willet, and other people involved. I tried unsuccessfully to find Claire Ahlquist several years ago, and would be glad to hear of her. Also, Kathy Karis. And I am curious about others.

I am still living in NYC — rather reluctantly, but in a "cheap" rent-stabilized apartment on the Lower East Side and in some ways it is a kind of a "trap" as the low rent makes it difficult to consider moving, but there have been huge changes in the neighborhood over the last 8 years with very rapid gentrification and I suppose some of it is welcome, but it did little for long-term residents except to make landlords more greedy and aggressive toward tenants. There has been quite an exodus. It has not been an easy place to live over the long term, and David and myself would like to possibly relocate to the West Coast if we can manage it -- San Francisco where I lived after Willet for several years.

Yours, Dana

Hello Oakes,

It is a bit strange to have people "from the past" streaming into your present with a 30 year or so hiatus, but very nice that you are trying to facilitate some communication/ contact. I heard from Kathy, who I have to reply to yet, and I don't quite remember the "ghost story" but would like to hear it (or read it?). I also want to write to Claire.

Kathy's anecdote about the horse is what I recalled to Jim Ord, minus the frostbite, but I do remember that we had a bit of a sense of panic/reality check about trying to stay up there for the winter with minimal support available -- it was a pretty wacky idea, with our level of country "subsistence" knowledge. We probably would have spent most of it in Willet's tavern if we had had any money! I think Kathy realized that she had better take care of what I think was a pretty valuable horse, and get it to a more comfortable place. So, off we went.

And I thought you would be still dealing with organic food/gardens/farming -- pretty satisfying actually. In Britain organic food is much more mainstream and as the farms are not quite so agri-business, they have some very tasty excellent produce, as well as meats and fruits and grains. It is a pleasure to go there and shop for food.

The barn was great! Not so great for the winter, but I remember some beautiful sunrises in the morning and a wonderful sense of safe, open space. I would love to have such a place now! And I was always impressed by your knowledge of bird songs -- another thing that is interesting in England -- as they take their birds seriously and many migrate through it, so I have learned a bit about sea birds which are evident in Cornwall.

Anyhow, if you do plan another Willet gathering (with maybe some more advanced notice?) keep me posted -- I think Jim was really up for it, and it would be interesting

to see people. Lucky Jarlath to have been able to stay up there, and travel around.
Sounds pretty luxurious.

Am glad to hear from you (!) and will check in again -- Best, Dana

Fall, 2008

Hello Oakes,

I did remember that you were about 38 years old, I think, that summer -- one of the
"older" people (!) and I was probably about 19 or 20? Hard to believe that you are 75,
and of course the older one gets the less old these numbers seem at least in your own
mind, until perhaps you look in the mirror! I hope you are staying healthy, and feeling
good. I know that your brother, George, passed away, because it was in the NY Times
and I thought of you at the time. Not easy to have members of your family "disappear"
as it were, and I am sorry.

I could not remember how Jarlath had arrived, but now I know. Did Craig Appel
live in your apt. building too? I have a vague memory of visiting someone in Boston
in late summer or fall, with I think Kathy again, and I believe it was connected with
you/someone you knew. Also, did not remember that you had kept a journal! I can
imagine some of the scenarios that are recollected in that?!? But I find it interesting
how some memories stay fresh and strong, and others just completely fade -- a mix of
subjective/emotional and objective facts. Of course, having a prompter in the form of a
journal does help sometimes to encourage your memory of associated events -- quite a
disciplined thing to do. Thanks for your journal entry and I would like to read more --

The barn was nice, and I vaguely recall the ghost story -- probably creaking in
the roof timbers from a temperature change (more than a ghost!) but I guess we all
wondered a bit what we were doing out there, rather than "in the house", which I am
sure just could not hold all of the folks there at that time. Not a lot of privacy. I don't
recall where I went after the barn -- and did not recall so many others were "sharing"
it (Claire for instance, who I remembered having her own room in the house!). David
Palmer actually visited me at Willet, having been to the Yukon (!) and back to the East
Coast en route to England in late October or November. I even hitch-hiked to Willet
from NYC, and was picked up just outside Binghamton by an old family friend (my
age) from Plattsburgh, NY who just happened to "drive by" and stopped -- one of those
bizarre coincidences that seem very strange! And that I would hitchhike around like
that kind of astounds me -- I don't remember relishing it very much, but I must have
felt if was a kind of rite of passage or something; either stupid or brave, or maybe both.

Anyhow, thanks -- interesting to think of those days again; I wrote back to Kathy
and still have to contact Claire -- keep me posted,

Fall, 2008

Hello again,

. . . For me, being at Willet raised questions of "how do I stay here?" -- what is my rightful place? -- am I cook, gardener, bottle washer, hand-maiden, or do I have some kind of "rightful position"? In the end I guess I did not feel that I had a rightful, independent position -- more of a guest position. Not any one person's fault, just kind of the problem with the structure of the place within the larger society. It is pretty hard to carve out these alternative spaces within the economic framework we have in the US. I was glad to participate in it for as long as I did, and wish that it had continued. It was a big project actually -- and not easy to determine a path.

I asked about Craig because he taught me how to make a French omelette, and I am very grateful. Also, I think he may have served us Kona coffee which was quite exotic at that time! (This is what I mean about the strange nature of "memory"). I hardly remember anything else, except wood floors in the apartment and that Craig was rather tall and fair-haired, intelligent, verbal and a bit depressed.

Thanks for the journal pages -- I like your writing and the descriptions are really lively and often make a picture for me. I almost remember sitting on that bench, that day (Enterprise's arrival) for instance! (probably sat on it often) and you coming downstream with all the "ladies" skinny-dipping makes me think of the Indian miniature paintings of Krishna and the cow maidens (he steals their clothes!). What a nice thing to have available to us for cooling off and relaxing! I also remember loving going to Cortland for an outing -- coffee shop and french fries, or apple pie or some such "bad" food as a little treat. Apart from buying farm materials. I also remember that that June was uncommonly wet -- maybe the start of the manifestation of global warming, with hindsight?

Whatever journal I might have had I don't know where it might be? That's too bad. I can't imagine that I would have kept up with it as well as you did, but I was especially interested in writing at that time.

Best, Dana

Messages from Jarlath Hamrock,
Willet's Present Owner

E-mails from Jarlath Hamrock telling about some Willet history, also personal history of his own, how he happened to stay out there all these years!!

Oakes, I haven't really given you much data re: how the farm at Willet actually became the AAM headquarters for New York State during the Jimmy Carter era in the late 1970s, and into the Reagan years of the early 1980s, when the radical American Agriculture Movement staged their infamous tractor-cades to Washington, D.C. in an effort to educate the American public about so-called "farm parity"—including various "save the family farm" schemes, legislative maneuvers to restrict lavish foreign investment in American farmland, initiating a national agricultural lands study, repealing the Carter-imposed Russian wheat embargo, promoting the beginnings of farm-related ethanol production, etc. (I remember one AAM slogan: "Bushels for Barrels"—the idea of regarding a bushel of wheat or rice or any other farm commodity as valuable, say, as a barrel of oil). On the other hand, these same outspoken farmers felt betrayed by Jimmy Carter, who called himself a farmer from Georgia, later supporting California's Ronald Reagan for president with their slogan: "In Carter we Trusted, Now we are Busted!" Not a lot of which went anywhere, in retrospect, politically.

But, one curious thing that did develop from that AAM association, remarkably, was when I gave testimony in Congress—with several other lobby groups in D.C. at the time—about the need for organic research at the USDA. It was the early 1980s. Organic production or research of any kind was taboo at the U.S. Department of Agriculture. Yet, the folks from Rodale Press, the Friends of the Earth, the National Resources Defense Council, NOFA, the "Save the Family Farm Coalition," among others — they desperately needed a general farm organization to rally behind their collective goal of getting the federal government to finally recognize "organics." The American Farm Bureau, the NFU (National Farmers Union), the National Grange, various commodity groups such as the American Corn Growers' Association, for example, and politically-strong national farm cooperative groups, none of them would touch organics, not even any of the land-grant universities. Only one farm organization at the time, surprisingly, the American Agriculture Movement, was willing—a bit reluctantly—to go along with their efforts. I recall distinctly how a handful of rather lefty organic lobbyists timidly trooped into the vociferous, you could say right-wing, AAM offices on Capitol Hill in the United Methodist Building on Maryland Avenue. After introducing them to several of the staff there, I brought them across the street over into the Supreme Court basement cafeteria where we had a little sit down. A deal was struck, that I would try to get the "OK" from AAM leaders at the time to agree to give testimony in support of organic research at USDA. It was during the heady, early months of Reagan's first slash-and-burn budget proposals, the annual four-year Farm Bill was making its way through the halls of Congress. I think you'll find my AAM testimony on record supporting organic research at USDA. As a result, something like a meager, if controversial, $10,000 grant was subsequently initiated at Beltsville, the USDA research center outside Washington, the very first of its kind. Now, of course, organic production is a household word, and nearly every land-grant college promotes organic research in some fashion or another. But few people today realize how the AAM, with its torturous banner of farm parity, was the hero thirty years ago behind getting the USDA to break the ice on organics. So, you could say the remains of "Willet Produce" was part of that early, pioneering initiative.

J.

Oakes: Yes, you are still a partner to Willet Produce—and Willet Produce is still intact somehow, though no longer producing vegetables, but as an entity. Not an active partner (ie: investment or time). Yet, a very important inactive partner. If you (and George and David Beach) hadn't taken the fiscal responsibility which then I took on when something had to be done somehow to "save" Willet from being sold, thirty years ago, Willet wouldn't be where it is today, basically preserved as a farm (albeit, not an organic farm). Development is rampant, and there is no doubt, at least in my mind, that the very attractive real estate that has become Willet today would have been sold down the river, developed somehow, probably a long time ago, in the late 70s, or 80s or 90s, or into the recent 21st century. Yee of little faith, is no moniker that can be associated with your effort at Willet, Oakes, because somehow evidently your faith in me to keep it on as a farm, at least in name, when development rules (and I've been lucky to handle this and the Ithaca-area farms, collectively) —well, your investment in Willet is still secure, if all these years preserving it as a farm was one of your goals.

Frankly, I have no aversion to seeing it develop again as some different kind of agricultural entity. But all these years now I have been too busy just staying alive (managing Willet and Chicken Coop, both). Truthfully, I am in the throes of having to "leave" it in good hands, after nearly 40 years of this. I would hate to see a golf course at Willet (ala your cousin Ames at Borderland), even one without housing (residential) attached to the scheme—a true golf course, without the ruffles. They don't exist anymore, they can't, the pressure to develop even the smallest 9-holer now, here in the United States, or in Scotland, doesn't matter, is too great. A golf course at Willet is not what the world needs. I have seen enough golf courses in my time, so I'm biased, and they don't impress me anymore, really. (Remember, my involvement in golf course design at Harvard was subterfuge, to organize an 18-hole project for Willet that might deter the NYS Low-Level Radioactive Waste Committee from choosing it as a nuclear dump site). Somehow I got into the business of being a tour caddy from it. But, I can see how some businessmen would love to play with the idea of developing Willet as a golf course, or an airport, a resort, on and on.

On the other hand, after 40 years, I have to nail down some kind of future arrangement for Willet. We can talk more about that when you arrive, as I hope George, Ira, and the rest do as well, around Labor Day. Let's hope it doesn't rain that weekend.

Adios, Jarlath

Oakes: As it worked out, I wouldn't have anything to do with paying off David Beach in any fashion, personally speaking, since he was incognito much of the time and I didn't have anything to do with him entering the financial scene to begin with; so George, who did, accepted that responsibility, and I accepted responsibility for paying off Oakes Plimpton, and everything else Willet Produce Inc. incurred, including corporate fiscal taxes that were never paid in Albany, the substantial mortgage, back land taxes, attorney fees, outstanding local bills, the works. George took title to the DuBois farm, I to the Crittenden farm. But the deal was, we both had options on the other's claim (first right of refusal), this way the farm might be brought back together. And several years, or soon after George returned from Persia with Alexa, sure enough he wanted to sell his share (the 115-acre DuBois portion) and I accepted his price, paid him in installments.

That was during the late 1970s, perhaps around 1977 when it was finalized. I bought Ira's shares of Willet Produce Inc. earlier on, when he wanted out, as well, down on Long Island. Truth is, Oakes, I still owe you $10,000 from that time, but you agreed it wasn't necessary to have me cover it right away—or at least around 1979, I think was the time frame—since expenses holding the farm together were subsequently too ponderous for me. But, all debts on the place were paid, essentially, except for that debt still owed you, by me. . . .

I did play golf naturally as a teenager, won the barely-coveted MVP (most valuable player award) in high school ('64, Garden City, NY), and then never bothered with the sport after that, not even in college. I guess I thought I sort of mastered the game as a kid, and other interests were surely more appealing in America in the 1960s than golf. But, when the radio-active dump fiasco reared its head around 1988 or so, I attended Harvard's Graduate School of Desgin, earning a certificate in golf design in an effort to keep the farm that was then the #3 rated site in New York State(!), designing 18 holes for the place as part of its defense "non-resident population," being part of the state's criteria. Long story short, the state didn't choose Cortland County after all for its low-level radioactive waste facility, instead building a facility in West Valley, N.Y., south of Buffalo. I then got back interested in the game again when my news director at WHCU told me to cover the B.C. Open in Binghamton. I caddied the event, and that was when I realized these professional tour caddies have a pretty amazing lifestyle, if they can manage to stay healthy enough, and on top of things mentally. It's a way to see the world. People take golf much too seriously, thinking the score is important, the swing, the etiquette and all that. Nine holes is certainly enough for one day, one morning or afternoon. 18 holes (four hours) is a lot of time to spend on a golf course! But that's what the pros do to compete, so it's quite consuming, professionally speaking. Just understanding that the landscape is something special, a park with trees and birds etc., after all, no matter how loud the greenies of the world may tell you that golf courses are heavy polluters, don't listen to them. Golf courses entail so much open space, so much green space. Now, the Audubon Society, for example, is partner to properly maintained country. . . .

Adios. Jarlath

Oakes: [I asked about Dan Mullins, the one other alternative person in Willet!]. Dan Mullins, who owns a small house on a hill near Cortland State College, had a disaster two weeks ago when a neo-Nazi kid torched it one night. He is now staying with a sort of nun friend of his in Homer. I invited him to Labor Day, but he was completely frazzled when I spoke with him in front of his ruinous, two-story, wood frame place on Pleasant Street. Curiously, if you drive by his old place in downtown Willet you will see it also was torched some time back and sits blackened from about a decade ago.

The Brown Beaver also sits in ruins (fire) at the corner, you will notice, from a year ago, so don't be shocked when you pull into the village. You be the best judge of how to get out to Willet. I take different venues and over the past 35 years it really depends on what business I have on the way. Seems like you are coming from Western Mass., so simply travel the interstate, or via Rt. 2, then Rt. 7 (the long way), through Albany, and from there it is a matter of whether you want to take I-88 (parallels Rt. 7) as far as, say, Oneonta, then travel west through the wilds of Chenango County, etc., or find I-81 South at Syracuse, quicker perhaps, if duller, but I have a reason to visit Syracuse as I have a girlfriend in the hood there. Weather determines, etc. Remember, Willet is really no place to grow vegetables. I think we learned that. (Still, I have nearly a $7000 tax bill to pay this season. Death and taxes, etc.)

Ciao J.

Jarlath raking the Kitchen Garden with Lori Wische,
photo by Jim Grossi

Journal Writer's Story

OK, back to the Journal writer — his life story: I must admit post Willet found me depressed, for here I was at age 40 with nothing accomplished as it were, too many friends of a different generation, no job, no prospects — what to do?? But gradually through therapy, finding a female partner (my present wife Pat Magee) and becoming a partner in a coffeehouse venture *Common Grounds* things started to look up. *Common Grounds* was on the balcony of *100 Flowers Bookstore* in Central Square, Cambridge. We served simple meals and drinks, coffee of course, and produced music on Friday nights (individual performers) and Sunday afternoons (groups), poetry Wednesday nights (not necessarily weekly).

Then I volunteered for the NEFCO Farm Crew at the Cambridge Food Co-op. The coordinator told me she was leaving for Thailand or somewhere the next week, would I be interested in taking over. *Yes!* We helped plant, cultivate, weed and harvest vegetables at local farms. In barter for our work the farmers gave a discount for the produce provided. Our principal farms were The Farm in Winchester and Harmony Farm in Reading. After a few years, the crews ceased — not enough volunteers. The Farm became a you-pick raspberry farm, and Harmony Farm got developed. . . The coffeehouse closed down when the bookstore went bankrupt — the summer of 1978. Yes we were there during the great blizzard of 1978 (which followed a heavy snowstorm the week before), tunneling our way down from 248 Brookline Street to Central Square to keep the coffeehouse and bookstore open!

In 1978 one day I received a note in my mailbox: *remember scout troupe #17??* I had volunteered in Law School at a settlement house in Roxbury, and the director talked me into running their scout troupe. My experience was limited, but I persevered, taking the kids camping (the Blue Hills, and five days one summer at Borderland), also teaching them knots, the Morse code, etc. We went swimming in the Harvard pool Saturdays. Philip Pierce, my former scout, now worked for Riverside Cambridgeport Redevelopment Corporation, and he was looking to go into business for himself. I was ready to move on from being a landlord, which I was not good at, either in collecting rent, setting up the rules, or in the many things a landlord has to know how to do. So a deal was struck! As a result of rent control, the value of the building was very low. I had purchased the building for $52,000 and put some $25,000 into it in rehabilitation. We set $78,000 for a price, and I had to give Phil a 2nd mortgage — the banks wouldn't finance it! Getting the building ready for him took a little doing. We had put together a 15 by 20 foot container garden up on the roof, pulling up the soil by rope — had to take that apart and remove it. Then my tenant Ace had talked me into letting him build a shack up on the roof (he left for a year and thus lost his apartment). He used the plumbing of the apartment below, and cadged their electricity. Thus he had light and could play records. He heated his shack with a home-made wood stove! Your cabin in the sky! Taking it down, the junk in a waste can somehow caught fire — very smoky, bringing the fire department to the building! They were not happy that I had allowed a shack to be built up there!!

We bought a house in Somerville near Ball Square — the neighbors gave us flowers as a welcoming present. We got to know all our neighbors better when our son Robin was born in 1981. There were perhaps five kids on our block, and I was the only adult who ever played with them. A man who grew up on our street returned to live there — he told us that when he was a kid, there were a 100 kids just on that one block!!

When the farm crews ended, I joined Nesenkeag Cooperative Farm in Litchfield, N. H. as a volunteer and soon became its volunteer coordinator and secretary, also fund raiser. They brought their produce down to Boston Public Housing projects to market at wholesale prices or below, coordinated through Boston Urban Gardeners. Then we would take inner city groups up to volunteer at the farm — in my mini-van! We would take a break and swim in the Merrimack, now cleaned up, though of course with bathing suits on.

Around this time too, 1986, the City of Somerville was looking for someone to restart the farmers market in Union Square — I volunteered, my wife Pat having been involved in its starting back in 1981. Interestingly both Cambridge and Somerville's markets were started by anti-poverty agencies, the concept being to bring fresh produce directly to the people for less, as the middleman would be eliminated. We moved the Market to Davis Square in 1990 or 91. And about that time I ended up managing the Cambridge market in Central Square as well. I also worked with the Somerville Community Corporation with Project Soup, the city food pantry, and as a volunteer advocating for consumers rights — also mediating. You may read through the lines here that I didn't have to work for a living — as the saving goes, a Trust Fund bum!

Leaving Nesenkeag Farm I became involved as a volunteer with Food For Free, leading crews out to glean or rescue crops left in the fields by farmers. Late in the season after the markets and stands are closed, perhaps frost slightly damaging the cabbages, it is not worth the farmer's while to harvest. Food For Free also went to the Chelsea Produce Market and various supermarkets to glean produce seconds and else, and then distributing to area food pantries and shelters. Ari Kurtz, a new age farmer out in Lincoln, determined to set aside an acre to grow greens (collards and kale) for Food For Free. At that time it was harder to find greens in the supermarkets. I helped to coordinate that project, bringing volunteers out there to work on Field of Greens as we came to call it.

We also gleaned produce from Parker Farm, then located on a rented field at the Gore Estate in Waltham. Steve Parker, the farmer, determined to move his farm to the Lyman Estate, also in Waltham, and a group of us thought perhaps we could start a non-profit farm at Gore. But the soil wasn't great and no irrigation, so when we heard there was a fallow field at the UMass Field Station, also in Waltham, better soil and irrigation hook ups, we put in a proposal and were accepted!

I wanted to call the new farm Warren Fields Community Farm after Cornelia Warren who had originally donated her farm to the University as a field station, but other heads prevailed to call it Waltham Fields, and we were off ! Four acres to till and plant! I persuaded my mother to give $5,000 to the new project, we incorporated as a non-profit *Community Farms Outreach* (we might start other farms, or help save them), and we hired Steve Ronan, my fellow gleaner, as our first farm hand. Eliot Coleman wrote that you could farm 5 acres with a rototiller — not so easy! We borrowed Steve Parker's tractor.

We planned to donate all of our produce to charity, but that proved impractical. Hearing about Community Supported Agriculture, we hired Tim Cooke, an experienced farmer, as our first farm manager, and we started a CSA, where people invest in their summer and fall's weekly delivery of produce up front. Then we approached foundations to support our model and charitable farm — we donated about half of our produce, and started a market similar to Nesenkeag's at the local public housing in Waltham. We found project residents to manage the market, selling cherry tomatoes for a penny each, etc., but we gradually came around to selling the produce at $2 a large grocery bag. We buttressed the Waltham Fields produce with seconds donated by the farmers at the market I managed. Around this time I had left managing the two farmers' markets in order to concentrate on my farm project. The Federation of Farmers Markets took them over. But a senior citizen who wanted to start a farmers market in Arlington, where we had moved in 1987, found out about me. This was 1997. And before I knew it I was starting a market there, which I managed until 2009.

Presently, a more professional team runs Waltham Fields, leaving me to new endeavors. Writing was one avenue as witness this book (!). We bought a house in

Arlington Heights when we moved, next to a park known as Robbins Farm, about 11 acres of open land (all grass) with a playground, a baseball field and now abandoned tennis courts, and a view of the Boston basin from Revere Beach to the Blue Hills, the entire skyline! I asked an elderly couple walking by our house what Robbins Farm was, and they remembered it as a farm! As I had time, I procured a tape recorder to record their story — the farmer Nathan Robbins invited them onto the farm to pick carrots for their daughter, later to let her ride the farm horse, etc. He also delivered milk and eggs. He lived in a mansion (the Robbins sisters, his first cousins, gave the town its library and town hall — inheritance from the grandfather Nathan Robbins who ran a produce and meats stall at Haymarket in Boston). He was estranged from his wife May — she lived in the front with electricity, he lived in the back with kerosene lamps — they didn't talk to each other, just wrote notes! The first interview lead to others, and research at the Library and old issues of the local paper filled out the story of its becoming a park. You can read all about it at the Robbins Library, or by purchasing the book, *Robbins Farm Park, a Local History* through Friends of Robbins Farm (or myself) key <*www.robbinsfarmpark.org*>.

This led to more writing projects, for I found at the local history room in the Library an oral history of the town done in the early 1970s transcribed in a loose leaf notebook, some 480 pages, fascinating accounts of life with horses, the invention of the automobile, silent movies, the telephone, etc., the volunteer fire department, the ice business on Spy Pond, and all the farms — 60 farms once in town (none now), 100 acres under glass, Italian women workers walking to the trolley carrying seconds produce on their heads and singing songs! The Arlington Arts Council sponsored the project, and we put together a book *Stories of Early 20th Century Life, An Oral History of Arlington* which you can obtain through the Arlington Historical Society or, again myself (many copies in my attic).

I thought to travel out to the farms which attended the Arlington Market, to interview the farmers and take photographs of the farms, which led to another book: *Farms and Farmers of the Arlington Farmers' Market 1997 - 2005.* I also included the farm chapter from the *Stories* book. These books were all self-published through the Penobscot Press in Maine. I marketed the books through local stores in town, such as the Five and Dime, the drugstore, the bakery, the copy shop, the bookstore of course, the farmers market. The Robbins Farm book sold out (1,000 copies); now there's a 3rd edition, each one with new additions — 2007!

My very latest book project was to reprint *Orchids at Christmas* a collection of essays about my grandfather, Oakes Ames, a botanist specializing in orchids, who headed the Botanical Museum at Harvard (now Natural History Museum) for many years. The booklet features my grandmother Blanche Ames's etchings and pen and ink drawings of orchids — which they sent out as holiday cards from 1937 to 1949 together with a poem — Wordsworth, Whitman, Browning, also some Twain, Thackeray, Darwin prose. In the reprint I added a photograph of my grandparents sawing wood out at Borderland in 1906, and a story by my grandfather of finding a lost orchid on a mountain in Brazil. A friend helped me register it at *Amazon.com*.

No, I never joined a country club or moved to the true suburbs. I still play tennis occasionally, more so when I played with my son growing up. I still swim in rivers and lakes with my wife Pat — often on day canoe trips. For exercise I try to bicycle and walk everywhere. In the winter I cross country ski and pond skate. Birding is a life-long hobby.

I'm still involved in farming, for after leaving Waltham Fields I called up a few farms to see if they had extra crops to glean, and the first one I called, Apple Field farm in Stowe, they had 4 rows of over-ripe beets they weren't going to harvest! I had an intrepid volunteer to help me, who was from Greece, Marina Mountraki, in her 60s, but plenty of stamina! I paid her a little to supplement her pension. Nearby Hmong Farm, at Bolton Flats, a southeast Asian immigrant experimental farm supported by Tufts, they had a whole field of unharvested winter squash, for the Cambodians and Laotians just use the leaves and tendrils. Two whole vanloads we gleaned from there. (The field flooded the next two seasons, and now they sell their winter squash!). Anyway, to make a long story short, I found myself a partner, and last year we incorporated the gleaning project as a non-profit! Check out our website at *www.bostonareagleaners. org*.

We are planning a 36th reunion of Willet Produce Farm this coming Labor Day, September 1st, 2008, and the Cambridge group may convene too over a late fall weekend. How will it be to see each other after 36 years have passed??

Willet Reunion Labor Day Weekend 2008

Present: George Jacobs with daughter Annie and partner Pat, Jill Jacobs with son Zhen, Ira Karasick with son Max, Jim Ord, Jarlath Hamrock with a woman friend Jill, Dan Keller with Frans Leenders who happened to be visiting from Holland, some friends of Dan and Ira from Mass., Oakes Plimpton; unfortunately Claire Alquist Gardam, Dana Wilner and Kathy Karis couldn't come.

The road not taken! Well, Jarlath did, and we are all in admiration of his staying power! I wondered what we would all do and whether we could relate to Willet, what it would be like to see everyone again. But Willet was beautiful, even the old house and barn and tractors, it was cool to see everyone again, and such tales from George and Jim and Dan and Frans! And the next generation was present with Ira's son Max and Jill's son Zhen, and George's daughter Annie and partner Pat. Jarlath gave Max and Zhen rides in the tractor to introduce them to the farm, and Max was won over, throwing his hat out the car window as they were leaving so they wouldn't have to leave!

We had perfect weather, and the stars and milky-way were a perfect show at night! Warm and sunny in the day to go swimming in Jarlath's farm ponds and to walk the fields and woods — the one farm pond is way in the back of the old buckwheat field. Cool to walk way up the hill onto a neighboring farm, some of the fields where hawthorn trees grew all grown over now with bushes and trees. Only Jarlath and I tried the river, very cold, and you had to bushwack, and transverse two barbed wire fences and an electric one. George had Annie send us a message to bring bathing suits, but the first day he himself swam without, with Frans, but mostly we swam with suits.

We were thankful to Jim for bringing and setting up an outside table and the fire grill, and both Jim and George helped Jarlath clean up for all of us. Dan brought Wendell grass-fed beef, and others brought veggies, tomatoes, etc., so we feasted well! We had beer of course, and even some red wine. Unfortunately Jim lost his one joint down the well! Jill, Jarlath's new friend from Cortland, was a great addition, helping Jarlath set up and bringing two tents with sleeping bags and pads — myself saved from putting up my tent at night and freezing in a very light blanket sleeping bag. Drumming into the night was something! George brought the drums and noise-makers, which we passed around, and George and Annie led us in a few chants. Later in the night and early morning the coyotes gave a few 'chants,' howling in chorus!

Of farming, all the fields are planted in field corn by a neighboring farmer, who just declared bankruptcy, so recompense doubtful. But a New York Organic Farming Assoc. ad has connected Jarlath with an organic beef farmer from across the valley who is interested in leasing Willet to grow hay, which everyone agrees would be the best land use. Jarlath pays his bills from such rentals, and from (would you believe) gas leases at $50 an acre for five years — 350 acres is the farm. He also collects minor money from hunting leases. Taxes are high at $8,000 a year. Jarlath sees himself as a farm preservationist — he has a small farm in Hector, N.Y. too! We talked of setting up a Willet Retreat Foundation — a place people could come to to chill out. Jim talked of using the spruce trees at the pine grove to build a log cabin where the horse barn once was (was his vocation). But, more practically, how about an annual reunion over Labor Day we all agreed! There is thought of having a reunion in October this fall for people who came out to Willet later in time from Brookline Street, Cambridge. Franz asked on the way back to Wendell (and Arlington for me) what was the connection — back to the earth, to nature, to a simpler and more basic life style, to each other!

Addendum

The lines above were written in September, 2008. Now it is December, 2010. As it happened we did not have another reunion out at Willet, but we have stayed in touch as you may imagine from leafing through this account of those times! As you may see I self-published through *iUniverse* publishing, which is a digital printer — less expensive by a half from regular printing, and you can order on demand, no 1,000 books in my attic!

Aside from the principals, I did have a few friends read through the manuscript to make editorial suggestions, not all of which I followed. I'm particularly thankful to Phil Lewis for some of his clarifying suggestions. Sarah Aubrey also read through the book, and my wife Pat Magee made suggestions as well. Thank you to iUniverse Press for their patience and expertise! You can communicate with me about Willet or else — my street address is 67 Coolidge Road, Arlington, MA 02476, e-mail address plimag@ comcast.net.

Oakes Plimpton, December 2010

REUNION PHOTO ALBUM

Frans, Ira and George!

Above: George and Jim at the Well; Below: Swimming at the Farm Pond!

120

My Ancient Self at the Barn 'Window'

Please turn page for the Addendum

In response to notice about the Journal book, a friend wrote me asking if I referenced the Nearings — *Living the Good Life* — Helen and Scott Nearing. Good question. In answer I thought I should add to my account thoughts on how we fit into over-all back-to-the-land movement. As it happened I was at the farm at Montague when the Nearings visited there. I have this vivid mental picture of them out there in the strawberry field picking berries, with straw hats for sun protection. Then a few months later, perhaps in the late fall 1973, they came to Boston, and we all trooped into the public TV studio for an interview show where the theme was the Nearings (the old) with the alternative communards of the new. I remember Sam Lovejoy, who had cut the cables to topple the 500 foot nuclear weather tower erected in Montague, was a principal spokesperson. I wrote Dan Keller to see if he remembered. Here is his reply:

Hi Oakes—Yes I was there, our band (Mungo's Marauders?) played on the show and the camera focused on the hole in my sock as my foot worked the bass drum pedal-¬I'm sure my mother loved that.

We churned butter and it coalesced just as the show ended—it was the Sonya Hamlin show, and yes Sam did most of the talking.

That's about all my humble memory can call up. xxx Dan

Wendell and Montague farms came closer to the Nearing model than Willet, for George and Ira and Jim left to start a serious farming venture, organic to be sure, but definitely a commercial venture. The Nearing's routine was very disciplined — dividing the day into subsistence farm work, civic work (helping humanity) and recreation (often music) or work bringing economic return. Scott very much believed in manual labor — building their own homes, etc.

Henry David Thoreau, the progenitor of the back-to-the-land movement, was critical of the local farmers, for he felt they worked far too hard, and did not appreciate the beauty of nature, nor did they ever recreate. No environmental or civic conscious¬ness. At Willet we did try hard to take a day off a week, and at least some of us took nature walks, and then we swam in the river, and played volleyball at night (Ira's camp). We also strove to be self-sufficient, fixing our own tractors, also the plumbing, and rehabbing our ancient house. We did not cut down our woodlot!

Civic work? Well not so much at Willet, until Jarlath took up the cause of the American Agriculture movement. But Wendell and Montague were seriously into the anti-nuclear movement — toppling the tower, protesting Seabrook Nuclear plans, and the Montague people put out *No Nukes — Everyone's Guide to Nuclear Power*, Anna Gyorgy & friends, South End Press, Boston, 1979.

Well, that is the short answer. In the end our experiment failed, but I think the current organic farming movement has more promise, for it is not based on protest (Vietnam War, Nuclear power), so much as enthusiasm for organic farming... O.P.